CANON EOS 5D MARK IV USER GUIDE

DISCLAIMER

This book is intended solely as an educational and informational resource for users of the Canon EOS 5D Mark IV camera. The information contained herein is based on the author's experience, research, and understanding of the camera at the time of writing.

While every effort has been made to ensure accuracy and clarity, no guarantee is made that the information is complete, current, or error-free.

This publication is not affiliated with, endorsed by, sponsored by, or approved by Canon Inc. or any of its subsidiaries. All product names, trademarks, and registered trademarks mentioned in this book are the property of their respective owners and are used for identification purposes only.

Photography and videography involve technical equipment, software, and settings that may change due to firmware updates, third-party accessories, environmental conditions, or individual user skill levels.

The author and publisher assume no responsibility for errors, omissions, equipment damage, data loss, missed shots, or undesired results that may occur from the use or misuse of the information contained in this book. Readers are responsible for exercising their own judgment and caution when applying camera settings, performing firmware updates, cleaning equipment, or using accessories. Always follow official manufacturer instructions, safety guidelines, and best practices when operating photographic equipment.

This book does not provide professional, legal, technical repair, or manufacturer-certified advice. Any reliance on the information provided is strictly at the reader's own risk.

By reading and using this book, you acknowledge and agree that the author and publisher shall not be held liable for any direct, indirect, incidental, or consequential damages arising from the use of the material presented.

TABLE OF CONTENTS

INTRODUCTION

You hold in your hands one of the most capable and celebrated professional DSLRs ever created: the Canon EOS 5D Mark IV. It is a work horse a technological marvel built for precision and versatility. But this immense power comes with corresponding complexity.

The sheer number of menus, Custom Functions (C.Fn), and sophisticated autofocus configurations can quickly turn the excitement of a new camera into immediate frustration. You didn't invest in a professional tool to leave it locked in Automatic mode or to spend hours guessing which obscure setting controls your image quality.

This book is your direct path to mastery. It is not a dense, theoretical textbook, nor is it a simple list of specifications.

I break down complex camera functions into simple, actionable steps that you can follow with your camera in hand. My philosophy is simple: I show you what to adjust, explain why it matters, and instruct you on how to apply it in real-world scenarios.

Inside, I cover the critical foundations, ensuring that your camera is set up correctly from the very first day, eliminating future technical roadblocks. We then move methodically through the key pillars of professional photography:

Exposure Made Repeatable: Mastering the precise control of Aperture, Shutter Speed, and ISO to achieve consistently accurate brightness and creative effects, regardless of the lighting conditions.

Autofocus You Can Trust: Demystifying the sophisticated 61-point AF system, from setting up Back-Button Focus to utilizing the advanced AF Case system for flawless tracking of fast-moving subjects.

Customization and Efficiency: Learning how to customize the camera controls and save full configurations (C1, C2, C3) to match your specific shooting style, ensuring you spend less time menu-diving and more time creating.

Beyond Stills: Unlocking the full potential of the 5D Mark IV's video capabilities, including 4K recording, frame rate selection, and harnessing the power of Dual Pixel CMOS AF for smooth, cinematic focus pulling.

By the time you finish this guide, you won't simply know where the settings are you will understand how to use your Canon EOS 5D Mark IV with confidence, precision, and creative freedom.

HOW TO USE THIS BOOK

This guide is designed to be an operational manual, not a theoretical textbook. To maximize your learning speed and build genuine confidence with your Canon EOS 5D Mark IV, I recommend a hands-on, three-step approach rooted in the Show, Explain, and Apply philosophy.

Do NOT simply read this book away from your camera. Use it as a workbook that eliminates guesswork and enforces muscle memory.

Step 1: Read This First Establish the "Why"

Before diving into the detailed step-by-step instructions of any chapter, take a moment to read the introductory segment and the brief explanations for each setting.

My focus is clarity:

1. Show: I identify the specific dial, button, or menu location you need to adjust.

2. Explain: I tell you exactly why that setting exists and how the camera interprets it.

3. Apply: I provide a real-world scenario where you would use it.

Step 2: Do This With Your Camera in HandBuild Muscle Memory

This is the most critical step. Treat every section, particularly those in Chapters 1 through 7, as an immediate assignment.

When the text instructs you to go to the Red Shooting Menu Tab 1, immediately open the menu and navigate there.

When instructed to press the M-Fn button and rotate the Quick Control Dial, physically perform that action while looking through the viewfinder.

Configure the recommended settings (like Back-Button Focus or Custom Shooting Modes) and then leave them set that way.

The Canon 5D Mark IV is a sophisticated tool, and confident mastery comes from immediate, repetitive interaction.

By continually practicing, applying the concepts immediately, and relying on the structured reminders, you will quickly move beyond merely operating the Canon EOS 5D Mark IV to truly mastering its power.

CHAPTER 1

First-Day Setup Without Guesswork

Congratulations. You have an incredible photographic tool in your hands. The Canon EOS 5D Mark IV is a sophisticated instrument built for speed, durability, and uncompromising image quality. But before you can unlock its creative potential, you must first handle the mandatory technical groundwork.

The process of setting up a professional camera for the first time can feel overwhelming, but this chapter is designed to remove all guesswork. We are not just going to turn the camera on; we are going to establish the proper operational foundation. Getting these essential steps right from power management to firmware versions to memory card preparation is the single most effective way to eliminate technical frustration and confusing errors later in your workflow.

Think of this first chapter as building the engine for your photography. If the engine isn't properly installed and fueled, nothing else matters. We will ensure that your camera is running on the latest software, that your storage is optimized for speed and reliability, and that you know exactly which physical button does what.

This is a hands-on chapter. Please have your Canon EOS 5D Mark IV, a charged battery, and your memory cards ready. We are going beyond the owner's manual, focusing on best practices used by working professionals. By the time we finish this initial setup, your camera will be perfectly configured, allowing you to focus entirely on composition and light, not settings and failures. Let's dive in.

Essential Setup: Power, Cards, Firmware, and Formatting

The Canon EOS 5D Mark IV requires specific initial steps to ensure stable operation and optimal file integrity. Do not skip these steps, as proper formatting and power management prevent data loss and operational errors down the line.

1. Charging and Inserting the Battery

The 5D Mark IV uses the Canon LP-E6N rechargeable lithium-ion battery.

Step 1: Charge the Battery

Insert the LP-E6N battery into the dedicated battery charger supplied with the camera. The charging indicator light will typically glow orange while charging and turn green once the battery is fully charged. Always ensure the battery is at 100% capacity before attempting a firmware update or a long shoot.

Step 2: Insert the Battery

Locate the battery compartment on the bottom of the camera body. Flip the locking lever to release the door, and then open the door. Insert the LP-E6N battery with the electrical contacts facing inward and the orange lock lever depressed. Push the battery down until the orange lever springs up and locks the battery securely in place. Close the battery compartment door.

2. Checking and Updating Firmware

Firmware is the internal operating software of your camera. Keeping it updated ensures the best performance, compatibility with modern lenses and accessories, and fixes any reported bugs.

Step 1: Check Current Firmware Version

Turn the camera on and press the Menu button. Navigate to the Setup menu (the wrench icon). Scroll through the Setup tabs (typically Tab 5 or 6) until you find the "Firmware Version" setting. Note the current version displayed on the screen.

Step 2: Verify Latest Version

Visit the official Canon support website and search for the latest firmware release for the EOS 5D Mark IV. If your camera's version is older than the current version available online, an update is recommended.

Step 3: Initiate Update (If Necessary)

If an update is required, download the firmware file from Canon's website and follow their precise, detailed instructions. Crucially, the firmware file must be loaded onto a freshly formatted memory card, and the camera battery must be fully charged before starting the update process.

3. Inserting and Formatting Memory Cards

The Canon 5D Mark IV features dual card slots: Slot 1 is for CompactFlash (CF) cards, and Slot 2 is for SD/SDHC/SDXC cards. Utilizing both slots provides workflow flexibility and backup capability.

Step 1: Insert the Cards

Open the memory card compartment door on the right side of the camera body.

For the CF card (Slot 1), ensure the card is correctly oriented (usually label facing out or towards the back of the camera) and gently slide it into the slot. Do not apply force, as bent pins can destroy the card slot.

For the SD card (Slot 2), insert it until it clicks into place.

Close the card compartment door securely.

Step 2: Format the Cards (Essential Best Practice)

It is crucial to format memory cards in the camera before every major shoot, even if they were formatted previously on a computer or in another camera. This establishes the necessary file structure for the 5D Mark IV and ensures reliable recording.

Access the Menu system.

Navigate to the Setup menu (Wrench icon, typically Tab 1).

Select "Format card."

The camera will prompt you to select the card slot you wish to format (Card 1 or Card 2). Select the first card.

You will see the option for "Low-level format." While this takes slightly longer, it performs a deeper write operation that is highly recommended for maximizing card reliability and resolving fragmentation issues. Select "Low-level format" and press OK.

Repeat the formatting process for the second memory card.

WARNING: Formatting a card permanently erases all images and data on it. Ensure all important files are backed up before proceeding.

Navigating Buttons, Dials, Menus, and Displays with Confidence

To transition from merely holding the 5D Mark IV to confidently operating it, you must first master its topography.

This camera is designed for speed; the physical controls allow you to adjust critical settings without ever entering the main menu system.

This walkthrough is your guided tour of the controls you will use the most. Keep your camera in hand and perform each step as you read.

I. Mastering the Primary Control Dials

The 5D Mark IV utilizes two primary, large control dials that manage the Exposure Triangle (Aperture, Shutter Speed, ISO) depending on your selected shooting mode.

1. The Main Dial (M. Dial): Located on the top of the camera, directly behind the shutter button.

Use: In Shutter Priority (Tv) and Manual (M) modes, this dial typically controls the Shutter Speed.

Turn the Main Dial left or right to increase or decrease the value.

2. The Quick Control Dial (Q. Dial): The large, ridged wheel located on the back of the camera, surrounding the SET button.

Use: In Aperture Priority (Av) and Manual (M) modes, this dial typically controls the Aperture value (f-stop). In Av/Tv mode, it often controls Exposure Compensation.

Turn the Quick Control Dial left or right to open or close the aperture, or to adjust compensation.

II. Essential Function Buttons

A few buttons are vital for instant control and professional efficiency.

1. The AF-ON Button: Located on the upper right rear of the camera, easily accessed by the thumb.

Function: This button is dedicated solely to engaging autofocus. By default, pressing the shutter button half-way also focuses, but professionals often separate this function (Back-Button Focus) to the AF-ON button for greater control over focus tracking and recomposing.

2. The M-Fn Button (Multi-Function): Located on the top plate, just behind the Main Dial.

Function: This is a highly customizable button, but by default, it is often set to switch between focusing modes or to quickly access ISO control.

Press and hold the M-Fn button, and then turn either the Main Dial or the Quick Control Dial to cycle through its assigned functions (e.g., changing ISO without taking your eye from the viewfinder).

3. The SET Button: Located in the center of the Quick Control Dial.

Function: The SET button confirms selections within menus and acts as a shortcut button, most notably for activating the Quick Control Screen (Q Screen).

III. Accessing and Navigating the Main Menu

All deep camera settings are managed through the Main Menu system.

1. Accessing the Menu:

Press the MENU button, located on the upper left rear of the camera body.

2. Navigating Tabs and Pages:

The 5D Mark IV menu is organized into color-coded tabs (Red for Shooting, Blue for Playback, Yellow for Setup, Orange for Custom Functions, and Green for My Menu).

Use the Multi-controller (the small joystick near the AF-ON button) to move horizontally between these color tabs.

Once a tab is selected, use the Multi-controller or turn the Quick Control Dial to move vertically through the numbered pages within that tab (e.g., Shooting 1, Shooting 2, etc.).

3. Selecting and Adjusting Settings:

Use the Multi-controller to highlight the desired setting, then press the SET button to enter the adjustment screen.

Adjust the value, and press SET again to confirm and return to the menu list.

IV. Utilizing the Quick Control Screen (Q Screen)

The Q Screen is your most powerful tool for making multiple setting changes quickly without digging through the deep menu structure.

1. Activating the Q Screen:

Action: Press the Q button (located near the bottom right of the rear LCD). The large LCD screen will display a grid of frequently used settings, such as Metering Mode, White Balance, Image Quality, and Drive Mode.

2. Changing Settings on the Q Screen:

Use the Multi-controller (joystick) to select and highlight the setting box you wish to change (e.g., the White Balance icon).

Once highlighted, turn the Quick Control Dial or the Main Dial to cycle through the available options for that setting. You will see the results change immediately on the screen.

3. Exiting the Q Screen:

Action: Press the Q button again, or lightly press the shutter button halfway down.

V. Customizing the Display

The 5D Mark IV allows you to select which information is displayed on the main LCD screen when the camera is powered on but not in Live View.

1. Cycling Display Information:

Press the INFO button (located near the top right of the LCD, next to the MENU button).

Each press cycles through different display modes: Standard Shooting Information (graphical), Electronic Level + Shooting Information, and Blank Screen. Choose the mode that provides the most useful visual feedback for your needs.

CHAPTER 2

Exposure Made Simple and Repeatable

If there is one technical skill that separates confident photographers from hesitant ones, it is mastery over exposure. Exposure is not just about making the image bright enough; it is the art of controlling light, motion, and depth of field simultaneously.

When you achieve repeatable, accurate exposure, you move beyond the camera guessing what looks good and start telling the camera exactly what you intend to capture.

The relationship between the three pillars of exposure Aperture, Shutter Speed, and ISO is often called the Exposure Triangle, and it is frequently presented in a way that feels overwhelming.

This chapter demystifies that relationship entirely. We will abandon the theoretical textbooks and focus exclusively on the practical, hands-on application of these settings using the Canon EOS 5D Mark IV's specific dials, controls, and modes.

By the end of this foundational chapter, you will understand not just what each setting does individually, but how they must be balanced in every single scenario from freezing fast action in bright sunlight to capturing still portraits in ambient light. More importantly, you will learn the decisive steps needed to shift from relying on the camera's automatic modes to taking confident control using Aperture Priority (Av), Shutter Priority (Tv), and finally, full Manual (M) control.

Accurate exposure is not a lucky accident; it is a straightforward, repeatable equation. Let's start mastering the foundation of every great photograph.

Aperture, Shutter, and ISO

Exposure in photography is determined by the interplay of three core settings: Aperture, Shutter Speed, and ISO. They form the "Exposure Triangle." Changing one setting inevitably requires changing at least one of the others to maintain the same brightness. Mastering the effect of each setting is the key to moving beyond automatic modes.

Aperture (F-Stop)

Aperture controls the size of the opening in the lens. This dictates how much light reaches the sensor, but its primary creative function is controlling Depth of Field (DoF)the zone of acceptable sharpness in front of and behind the subject. A small f-number (like f/2.8) is a wide opening (shallow DoF); a large f-number (like f/16) is a narrow opening (deep DoF).

How to set it on the 5D IV: In Aperture Priority (Av) mode or Manual (M) mode, the Aperture is adjusted using the Main Dial, which is the dial located just behind the shutter button.

Why it matters in a real shooting scenario:

Portraits: Use a wide aperture (f/2.8 to f/5.6) to create a shallow DoF, ensuring the background is beautifully blurred (bokeh) and the subject stands out sharply.

Landscapes: Use a narrow aperture (f/11 to f/16) to achieve maximum depth of field, keeping everything from the immediate foreground to the distant horizon sharp.

Shutter Speed (Time)

Shutter Speed determines the length of time the camera's sensor is exposed to light. It is measured in fractions of a second (1/100, 1/250, etc.) or full seconds. Its primary creative function is controlling motion blur.

How to set it on the 5D IV: In Shutter Priority (Tv) mode or Manual (M) mode, Shutter Speed is adjusted using the Quick Control Dial, the large rotary dial located on the rear of the camera.

Why it matters in a real shooting scenario:

Freezing Action: For sports, wildlife, or children playing, use a very fast shutter speed (1/500 sec or faster) to freeze movement completely, ensuring sharp, crisp action.

Creating Movement: For artistic effects like smoothing water in a waterfall or capturing the light trails of cars at night, use a slow shutter speed (1/15 sec to several seconds). This requires a stable tripod to prevent camera shake.

ISO (Sensitivity)

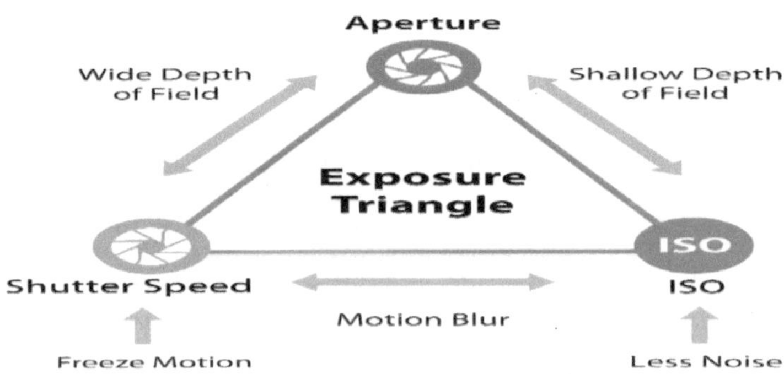

ISO controls the sensor's sensitivity to light. A lower ISO (e.g., 100) results in the cleanest image quality but requires more light. A higher ISO (e.g., 3200) amplifies the light signal digitally, allowing you to shoot in dark conditions, but introduces digital noise or "grain."

How to set it on the 5D IV: Press the dedicated ISO button (located on the top plate near the LCD screen) and adjust the value using either the Main Dial or the Quick Control Dial.

Why it matters in a real shooting scenario:

Maintaining Image Quality: Always aim to use the native or lowest possible ISO (ISO 100 is standard) when light is plentiful, such as outdoors on a sunny day, to ensure the cleanest, most detailed images.

Low Light Flexibility: If you must maintain a specific Aperture and Shutter Speed (e.g., 1/125 sec at f/4) but the light is too dim, increase the ISO (e.g., 1600 or 3200) as the last resort to properly expose the shot without blur.

The Exposure Triangle in Action

These three settings are interdependent. If you move your aperture from f/4 (wide) to f/11 (narrow) to deepen your depth of field, you reduce the light hitting the sensor significantly.

To compensate and maintain the same brightness, you must either slow down the Shutter Speed or increase the ISO. Successful exposure control is the rapid, intelligent balancing of these three variables to achieve both technical brightness and the desired creative effect.

When to Use Av, Tv, and Manual Mode

Aperture Priority (Av Mode)

Aperture Priority is arguably the most frequently used mode by intermediate and professional photographers because it prioritizes the single most powerful creative tool: depth of field.

How to Select It

Locate the Mode Dial on the top left of the camera body. Turn the dial until the indicator aligns with Av.

What It Controls

In Av mode, you set the Aperture (f-number), and the Canon 5D Mark IV automatically calculates and sets the corresponding Shutter Speed required to achieve a correct exposure, based on your chosen ISO.

When to Use It

Use Av mode exclusively when controlling the depth of fieldthe amount of the image that is in sharp focusis your primary creative concern.

Portraits and Headshots: Use wide apertures (small f-numbers like f/1.4 to f/4) to blur the background (bokeh), isolating the subject and making them pop.

Landscape Photography: Use narrow apertures (large f-numbers like f/8 to f/16) to maximize the depth of field, ensuring everything from the foreground to the distant horizon is sharp.

Macro Photography: This mode allows you to precisely dial in the very small apertures needed to maximize the limited depth of field inherent in close-up work.

Example Settings

Scenario: Classic Outdoor Portrait

Goal: Subject sharp, background soft.

Settings: Av mode, f/2.0 (or the widest your lens allows), ISO 100 (or Auto ISO). The camera selects the necessary shutter speed.

Scenario: Vast, Sunny Landscape

Goal: Maximum sharpness across the scene.

Settings: Av mode, f/11, ISO 100. The camera selects the necessary shutter speed.

Shutter Priority (Tv Mode)

Shutter Priority mode gives you absolute control over motion blur and freezing action, making it crucial for dynamic photography genres.

How to Select It

Turn the Mode Dial on the top left of the camera body until the indicator aligns with Tv.

What It Controls

In Tv mode, you set the Shutter Speed (e.g., 1/250s or 1/4s), and the 5D Mark IV automatically calculates and sets the appropriate Aperture (f-number) needed for correct exposure.

When to Use It

Use Tv mode exclusively when controlling motion is your primary concern. This includes freezing action or creating intentional motion blur.

Sports and Wildlife: Use fast shutter speeds (1/500s or faster) to freeze high-speed subjects like a bird in flight or a racing car.

Reporting: Use moderately fast speeds (1/125s to 1/250s) to reduce camera shake and blur in unpredictable environments.

Artistic Blur: Use slow shutter speeds (1/2s to 2 seconds) to intentionally blur moving water (waterfalls, streams) or clouds, creating a silky effect.

Example Settings

Scenario: Freezing a Runner or Moving Pet

Goal: Crystal-clear, frozen action.

Settings: Tv mode, 1/1000s, ISO 400 (or Auto ISO). The camera selects the necessary aperture.

Scenario: Silky Waterfalls

Goal: Smooth, blurred water flow. (Requires a tripod.)

Settings: Tv mode, 1/4 second, ISO 100. The camera selects the necessary aperture.

Manual Mode (M Mode)

Manual Mode grants the photographer full, independent control over all three exposure parameters: Aperture, Shutter Speed, and ISO.

How to Select It

Turn the Mode Dial on the top left of the camera body until the indicator aligns with M.

What It Controls

You must set the Aperture (using the Main Dial), the Shutter Speed (using the Quick Control Dial), and the ISO. The camera's internal light meter simply acts as a guide, displayed in the viewfinder or on the LCD panel, helping you confirm if your chosen settings are over- or under-exposing the scene.

When to Use It

Use Manual mode whenever absolute, repeatable consistency is needed, or when the lighting conditions are complex and confuse the camera's automatic metering system.

Studio Photography with Flash: Manual mode is essential here. You lock the settings (typically 1/125s, f/8, ISO 100) and rely on the external flash power to control the light, ensuring every shot is identical.

Changing Light Conditions (Sunrise/Sunset): When the light is rapidly changing, the camera's meter can be inconsistent. Manual mode allows you to lock in the perfect exposure and slowly adjust only one setting (usually the shutter speed) as the light fades.

Long Exposures and Night Photography: When shooting extremely long exposures (seconds or minutes), manual control is required to prevent overexposure and manage noise.

Example Settings

Scenario: Locked-Down Studio Portrait with Strobes

Goal: Consistent exposure across 50 shots.

Settings: M mode, f/8 (for sharpness and depth of field), 1/125s (standard flash sync speed), ISO 100 (lowest noise).

Scenario: Street Photography in Consistent Daylight

Goal: Predictable exposure when moving between shade and sun.

Settings: M mode, f/5.6 (controlling DoF), 1/500s (for sharpness), ISO 400.

Summary of Control

Mode	You Control	Camera Controls	Primary Goal
Av (Aperture Priority)	Aperture	Shutter Speed	Control Depth of Field
Tv (Shutter Priority)	Shutter Speed	Aperture	Control Motion
M (Manual)	Aperture & Shutter Speed & ISO	Nothing (Metering is only a guide)	Absolute Consistency and Complex Lighting

CHAPTER 3

Autofocus You Can Trust

The difference between a snapshot and a professional photograph often comes down to one non-negotiable factor: sharpness. No matter how perfect your composition or how accurate your exposure, if your subject is not critically sharp, the image fails. Reliable, repeatable focus is the secret weapon of confident photographers.

The Canon EOS 5D Mark IV is equipped with a formidable 61-point high-density reticular autofocus system. It is fast, flexible, and astonishingly accurate, but it is also complex. If you leave the system set to its factory defaults, you are relying on the camera to guess your intentions, which inevitably leads to missed focus, especially in challenging situations.

This chapter is your definitive guide to taming and customizing the core autofocus system. We will start by establishing the fundamentals necessary to achieve pin-sharp results with static subjects portraits, landscapes, and scenes where the subject remains still. Mastering this foundation is crucial; it ensures you understand how the camera achieves focus before we move on to the complexities of tracking moving action in the next chapter.

I will break down the crucial modes and controls you must configure immediately. By the time you finish this section, you will not just know where the focus points are; you will understand how to command them precisely, culminating in the essential, professional technique of setting up Back-Button Focus. Get ready to stop guessing and start guaranteeing sharpness.

One-Shot vs AI Servo-Choosing the Right AF Mode Every Time

One-Shot AF is the Canon EOS 5D Mark IV's default mode designed for subjects that are stationary. This mode operates under the principle of 'focus and lock.' Function and Behavior:

1. When you half-press the shutter button, the camera focuses on the selected AF point.
2. Once focus is achieved, the focusing system stops, a confirmation beep sounds (if enabled), and the chosen AF point illuminates green.

3. The focus distance is locked until you release the shutter button, allowing you to re-compose the shot while maintaining critical focus.

4. If the subject moves after focus is locked, the resulting image will be out of focus. When to Use One-Shot AF**:** Use One-Shot AF only when the subject is absolutely still and you are not moving your physical position in relation to the subject. Examples include:

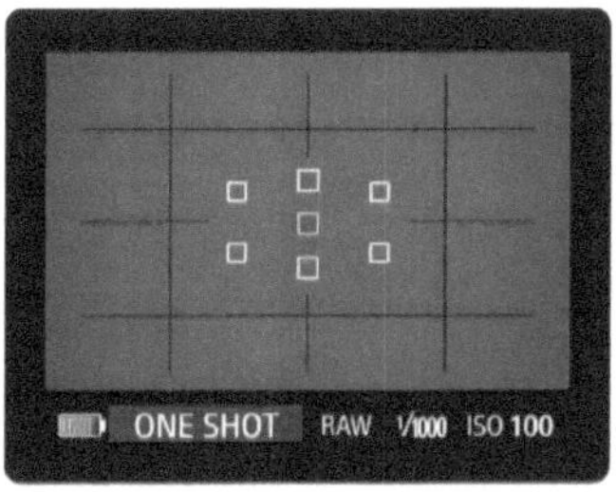

One-Shot AF

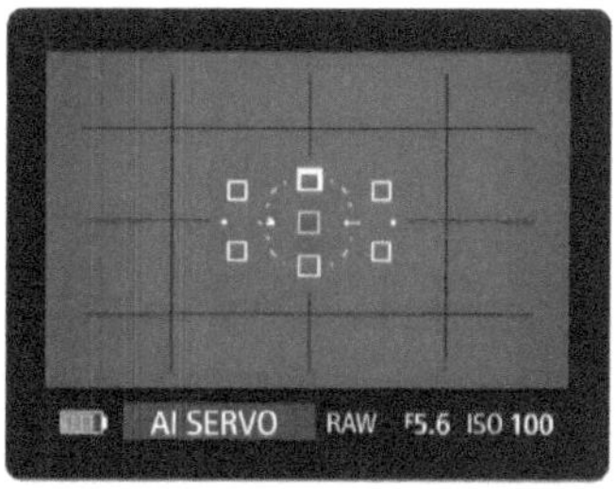

AI Servo AF

Landscapes

Still life and product photography

Portraits where the subject is holding a pose

Studio or architecture shots

AI Servo AF: The Moving Subject Tracker

AI Servo AF is the mode specifically engineered for tracking motion. This mode ensures that the focus constantly adjusts as the subject distance changes.

Function and Behavior:

1. When you half-press the shutter button, the camera begins continuous focusing on the selected AF point.

2. The camera's processor continually monitors the distance and predicts the subject's position at the moment the shutter will fire.

3. As long as you keep the shutter button half-pressed (or use Back-Button Focus), the 5D Mark IV will track the subject, adjusting focus distance multiple times per second.

4. In this mode, the camera prioritizes shutter release speed over confirmation. There is no focus lock or confirmation beep, allowing the camera to fire continuously for high-speed sequences.

When to Use AI Servo AF:

Use AI Servo AF for any subject that is moving, or when you, as the photographer, are moving and shifting the distance between the camera and the subject.

Examples include:

Sports and action photography

Wildlife in motion

Children and pets playing

Documentary or wedding photography where subjects are walking or dancing

Step-by-Step: Changing the AF Mode

The fastest way to switch between One-Shot and AI Servo is by using the dedicated AF point selection controls.

1. Access the Settings: Press the dedicated AF Point Selection button (located near the AF-ON button on the rear of the camera). This activates the AF settings display on the top LCD and the viewfinder.

2. Select AF Mode: While the settings display is active, use the M-Fn button (Multi-Function button, located directly behind the main command dial). Pressing M-Fn cycles through the primary AF settings (AF Area, AF Mode, etc.).

3. Adjust the Mode: Once the AF Mode icon is highlighted (it looks like a square or a box with two arrows), rotate the

Main Dial (the dial near the shutter button) to cycle through the options:

Single square icon = One-Shot AF

Box with two arrows icon = AI Servo AF

AI Focus icon (a mixture of the two, not recommended for critical professional work)

4. Confirm: Release the AF Point Selection button. The mode is instantly set.

Alternatively, you can access this setting via the Quick Control screen:

1. Press the Q button (Quick Control).

2. Navigate to the AF Mode icon (usually located on the bottom left of the screen).

3. Press SET or tap the icon to select your desired AF mode.

Focus Points, AF Areas, and Back-Button Focus Setup

The Canon EOS 5D Mark IV's 61-point AF system offers incredible precision, but it must be controlled strategically.

Mastering the use of specific focus points and area modes is essential before customizing the system with advanced techniques like Back-Button Focus (BBF).

AF Points and Area Selection Modes

The 5D Mark IV offers numerous ways to select which of the 61 points the camera uses to achieve focus. The primary tool for changing the selection mode is the AF Area Select button, typically used in conjunction with the M-Fn button or the Multi-controller (joystick).

Step-by-Step Selection

1. Press the AF Area Select button (located near the top display, next to the M-Fn button).

2. While looking through the viewfinder or at the top LCD, use the Main Dial (top right dial) or the M-Fn button to cycle through the available Area Selection Modes.

Key AF Area Modes and Usage:

Single-Point AF: This is the most precise mode. It uses only one chosen AF point.

Use when: Shooting stationary portraits, macro photography, or landscapes where focus must be placed precisely on a specific object (e.g., an eye or a single flower).

How to select the point: Once Single-Point is chosen, use the Multi-controller (joystick) to quickly move the active point anywhere within the 61-point grid.

Zone AF: This groups the 61 points into nine distinct zones. The camera will use any point within the selected zone.

Use when: Your subject is moving predictably but might stray slightly from the center (e.g., event coverage, pets playing). It is faster than single-point but maintains control over the general area of focus.

Large Zone AF: Similar to Zone AF, but divides the area into three much larger sections (left, center, right).

Use when: Shooting sports or fast-moving wildlife where the subject's movement is erratic, and you need quick, wide coverage without relying solely on automatic selection.

Automatic AF Point Selection: The camera takes control and selects the focus points based on distance, color, and contrast.

Use when: Capturing spontaneous moments when speed is critical and precision is secondary.

Implementing Back-Button Focus (BBF)

Back-Button Focus is the technique of separating the focusing action from the shutter release button. The shutter button (half-press) now only meters light and takes the picture; a dedicated button on the back (typically AF-ON or the AE Lock button) is used exclusively for focusing. This is considered an essential technique for professionals due to the control it provides, especially when switching between stationary and moving subjects.

Back-Button Focus Setup (C.Fn III-3)

1. Access the Main Menu: Press the Menu button and navigate to the Custom Functions (C.Fn) section (Orange/Yellow tab).

2. Select Custom Function III: Operation/Others.

3. Select C.Fn III-3: Custom Controls.

4. Configure the AF-ON Button:

Select the AF-ON icon (top right button on the back of the camera).

Set its function to: Metering + AF Start.

5. Configure the AE Lock () Button: (Optional, but useful for secondary AF control)

Select the AE Lock () icon.

Set its function to: AF Stop (or a similar non-focusing function).

6. Configure the Shutter Button (Half-Press):

Select the Shutter Button icon.

Set its function to: Metering Start. This is the crucial step that disables focusing via the half-press.

7. Save and Exit: Press the SET button and exit the menu.

Why Back-Button Focus is Essential

BBF gives you the power to instantly switch between One-Shot and AI Servo functionality without ever changing the camera's AF mode.

1. Focus and Recompose (Stationary Subjects): Set the camera to AI Servo. Press the AF-ON button to focus on your subject, then release the AF-ON button. The focus is now locked (like One-Shot mode). You can recompose the

shot, shoot multiple frames, and the focus distance will not change until you press AF-ON again.

2. Continuous Tracking (Moving Subjects): Keep the camera set to AI Servo. Hold down the AF-ON button continuously while tracking the subject. The camera will adjust focus until you take the shot.

3. Avoiding Refocusing: If a subject briefly stops moving, you can simply release the AF-ON button, take the photo, and the focus remains locked. The camera will not hunt or refocus when you half-press the shutter.

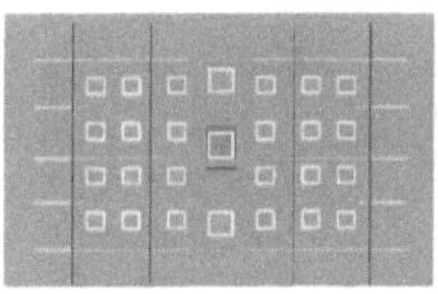

Single-Point AF

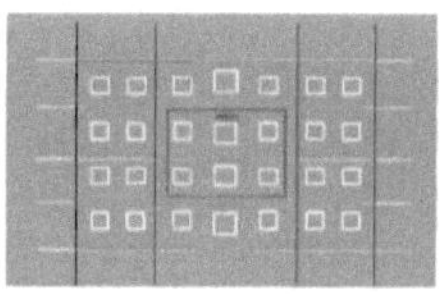

Zone AF

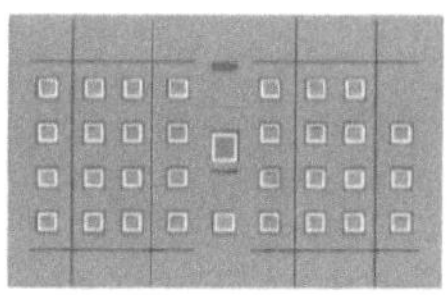

Automatic Selection

Canon
EOS
Canon

CHAPTER 4

Advanced Autofocus for Moving Subjects

The transition from reliably focusing on a static subject to tracking a subject moving at speed or erratically is often the biggest hurdle in action photography. In dynamic environments whether you are capturing a wedding dance, a fast-paced sporting event, or unpredictable wildlife a simple "hold-and-hope" approach to autofocus will yield an unacceptable number of missed shots. This chapter is your definitive guide to mastering movement, transforming the Canon EOS 5D Mark IV into a relentless, precise tracking machine.

The key to unlocking the 5D Mark IV's incredible potential for dynamic subjects lies within the sophisticated Autofocus (AF) Case system. These pre-configured and customizable presets adjust the camera's internal algorithm show quickly it reacts to obstacles, how aggressively it tracks accelerating subjects, and how it handles momentary loss of focus. Without selecting and tailoring the correct AF Case, you are asking a powerful computer to guess your intentions; with proper configuration, you are programming it for success.

We will move beyond the basic AI Servo setting and explore how to apply specific AF Cases designed for subjects that change speed, cross behind obstructions, or move totally unpredictably.

Mastering this system, along with the subsequent fine-tuning parameters, ensures that focus is not merely an afterthought, but a reliable, repeatable certainty, even when the action is happening faster than you can consciously react. The goal is simple: eliminate technical failure and ensure that every peak moment of action is captured with absolute sharpness.

Understanding AF Case Settings and Tracking Behavior

The 5D Mark IV's Autofocus Case system is your most powerful tool for achieving sharp focus on moving subjects. It allows you to pre-program the camera's tracking logic to match the movement of your subject, eliminating the need to manually adjust complex settings while shooting.

The system relies on three core parameters Tracking Sensitivity, Acceleration/Deceleration Tracking, and AF Point Auto Switching. Canon has grouped optimized values for these parameters into six predefined cases.

To access and select an AF Case:

1. Press the MENU button.

2. Navigate to the red Autofocus (AF) tab.

3. Select the third menu screen (AF 3).

4. Choose AF function (Case 1–6).

5. Scroll through the options and press SET to confirm.

AF Case Breakdowns

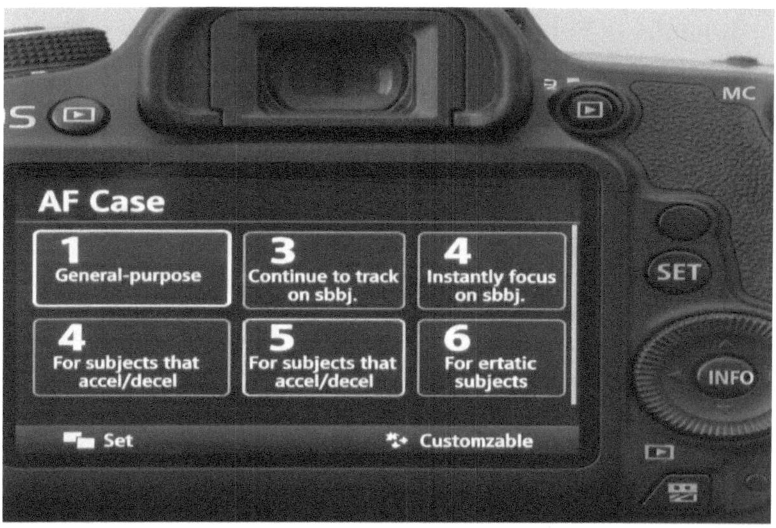

Case 1: Versatile Multi-Purpose Setting

Description: This is the default, balanced setting. It handles steady, predictable movement with moderate sensitivity and equal response to acceleration. It is designed to work well for the widest variety of scenarios without specific customization.

Optimal Scenario: Subjects moving at a uniform speed, such as a runner on a straight track, a person walking, or a vehicle traveling at a constant speed.

Case 2: Continue to Track Subjects, Ignoring Potential Obstacles

Description: This case reduces the Tracking Sensitivity parameter. This instructs the camera to intentionally ignore brief interruptions (like a fence post, tree, or referee) that might momentarily block the focus point. The camera prioritizes the original subject, assuming it will reappear quickly.

Optimal Scenario: Team sports (soccer, basketball) where one player might block another, shooting wildlife through light foliage, or scenes where transient elements cross the frame.

Case 3: Instantaneously Focus on Subjects that Enter AF Points

Description: This is the opposite of Case 2. Tracking Sensitivity is highly increased. The camera will immediately shift focus to any new subject that enters the selected AF area. Use this when you expect quick changes in subject distance or when you need to switch focus rapidly between nearby objects.

Optimal Scenario: Shooting subjects that stop and start suddenly, such as subjects emerging quickly from a tunnel, high-speed starts in a race, or subjects entering the frame unexpectedly.

Case 4: For Subjects that Accelerate or Decelerate Quickly

Description: This case optimizes the Acceleration/Deceleration Tracking parameter, making the system extremely responsive to changes in the subject's speed moving toward or away from the camera. If your subject changes velocity rapidly, this case is essential.

Optimal Scenario: Motorsport where vehicles brake hard into a turn and accelerate out, birds taking flight or landing, or subjects moving erratically toward the camera.

Case 5: For Erratic Subjects Moving Up, Down, and Side to Side

Description: Case 5 focuses on improving the AF Point Auto Switching parameter. When using Zone AF or Automatic AF Point Selection, this setting helps the focus points follow a subject that moves quickly and unpredictably across the focus area (vertical and horizontal movement).

Optimal Scenario: Gymnastics, dancers, birds or small animals exhibiting highly erratic movements in unpredictable patterns.

Case 6: Case Settings Determined by User

Description: This is the fully manual configuration mode. Selecting Case 6 does not immediately change settings, but it unlocks the three primary parameters for individual adjustment, allowing you to create a specific profile tailored precisely to a unique scenario that no other preset handles effectively.

Optimal Scenario: When you have experimented with Cases 1–5 and still find the performance suboptimal, or when you have a specific, recurring shooting situation (e.g., a specific sport venue with unique lighting) that requires fine-tuning.

Fine-Tuning Sensitivity, Acceleration, and Priority

These three fine-tuning parameters determine the actual behavior of the AI Servo system, regardless of which Case (1-6) you initially select. Adjusting these settings allows you to customize a generic Case to perfectly match the speed and unpredictability of your specific subject.

To access these controls:

1. Press the Menu button.

2. Navigate to the AF Tab (red camera icon).

3. Select AF 1, then AF Configuration Tool.

4. Select the Case you wish to modify (or the preset Case 1 if starting fresh).

Tracking Sensitivity (AI Servo tracking sensitivity)

This parameter controls how quickly the camera's autofocus system reacts to changes in subject distance. It dictates whether the camera should instantly refocus when a new object appears or if it should deliberately ignore brief obstructions.

Setting the Parameter:

The scale ranges from -2 (Locked On) to +2 (Responsive).

Real-World Application:

Move toward Locked On (-2, -1): Use this setting when your subject is likely to be briefly obstructed by obstaclesa runner passing behind a hurdle, a basketball player behind a referee, or wildlife momentarily obscured by brush.

By setting it to Locked On, the camera assumes the subject has not moved and holds the existing focus distance, preventing the focus from snapping to the obstruction.

Move toward Responsive (+1, +2): Use this setting when you are shooting a dynamic scene where subjects quickly enter and exit the frame or when you are frequently changing focus between subjects at widely different distances (e.g., street photography, event coverage).

The camera will immediately hunt for and establish focus on the new, dominant subject.

Acceleration/Deceleration Tracking

This parameter dictates how the camera responds when the subject's speed changes rapidly (speeding up or slowing down). This is critical because the AI Servo system relies on predicting where the subject will be when the shutter opens; speed changes throw off those predictions.

Setting the Parameter:

The scale ranges from 0 (Slow) to 2 (Fast).

Real-World Application:

Move toward Slow (0): Use when tracking subjects with highly predictable, constant movement, such as an aircraft in a straight line or a long-distance runner maintaining a steady pace. This avoids over-correcting for minor speed variations.

Move toward Fast (1, 2): Use for subjects that are erratic and change speed aggressively, such as a soccer player cutting, a bird taking flight, or any action that involves sharp, sudden acceleration or deceleration.

Setting this to Fast helps the AF system catch up with the rapid changes in prediction required.

AF Point Auto Switching

This parameter only applies when you are using an AF Area Selection Mode that utilizes multiple focus points (like Zone AF, Large Zone AF, or Auto Selection AF). It controls the speed at which the camera switches the active focus point to follow the subject across the chosen AF area.

Setting the Parameter:

The scale ranges from 0 (Slow) to 2 (Fast).

Real-World Application:

Move toward Slow (0): Use when you are tracking a subject within a controlled space, and you want the camera to be deliberate about switching focus points. This provides slightly greater precision by limiting the system's eagerness to jump to adjacent points.

Move toward Fast (1, 2): Use when the subject is small, fast, and moving unpredictably across the active AF area (e.g., small birds in flight or motocross). A Fast setting ensures the AF system quickly hands off tracking from one point to the next to maintain coverage, minimizing the chance of losing the subject entirely.

CHAPTER 5

Consistent Color, Light, and Image Quality

Technical mastery is not measured by the quality of one isolated photograph, but by the consistency and technical fidelity of an entire body of work. Light and color are the two most elusive variables in photography, constantly shifting with the environment. If you cannot rely on your camera to capture accurate color and optimal light exposure repeatedly, technical frustration quickly follows.

This chapter shifts focus from pure mechanical control (exposure and focus) to the critical internal processing tools that guarantee image quality and consistency directly within the camera. The Canon EOS 5D Mark IV provides sophisticated systems designed to eliminate guesswork, allowing you to achieve accurate representation of a scene whether you are shooting under harsh midday sun, tungsten indoor lighting, or deep twilight.

I will demystify the critical relationship between metering modes the camera's primary method for analyzing and interpreting light and White Balance settings, which dictates how the camera interprets and renders color temperature. Learning how and when to switch from Evaluative to Spot metering, or how to quickly set a Custom White Balance, is essential for repeatable, professional results.

Furthermore, I will address the challenges of low-light performance. The ability of the 5D Mark IV to produce clean, usable images at high ISO settings is a significant advantage, but it requires careful configuration of noise reduction parameters and ISO limits. By mastering the controls detailed in this chapter, you will transform unpredictable, variable captures into a stream of technically consistent images, providing the perfect foundation for any post-processing workflow.

Metering Modes and White Balance for Accurate Results

The metering mode determines how the Canon EOS 5D Mark IV measures the light in a scene to calculate the correct exposure. Choosing the appropriate mode is crucial for consistent results, especially in challenging, high-contrast environments.

Step-by-Step: Selecting Your Metering Mode

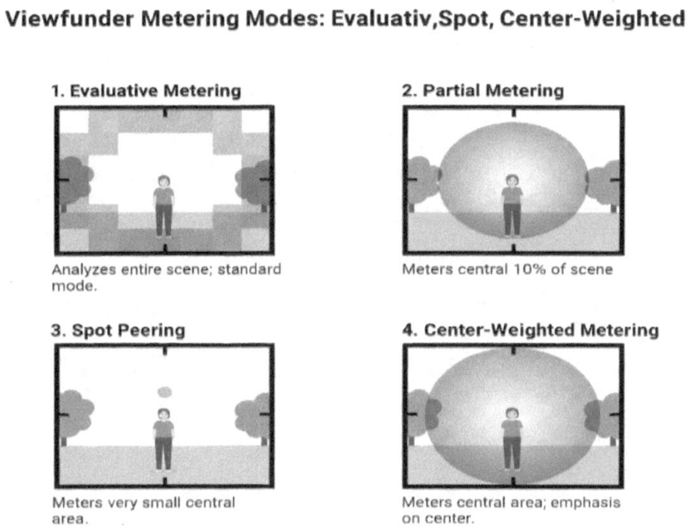

1. Press the Metering Mode selection button (often accessed via the M-Fn button or the Quick Control Screen).

2. Rotate the Main Dial or Quick Control Dial until the desired icon appears on the top LCD or in the viewfinder.

The Four Metering Modes and Their Applications

1. Evaluative Metering (Icon: A square with a small circle)

This is the default mode. It divides the scene into numerous zones, analyzes light levels, contrast, and color, and prioritizes the area covered by the active autofocus point. It aims to achieve an overall balanced exposure.

When to use it: Approximately 90% of the time. Use for landscapes, group photos, and general shooting conditions where the lighting is relatively even or the subject is not severely backlit.

2. Partial Metering (Icon: A circle in the center, smaller than Spot)

Measures only a small central area of the frame (about 6.2% of the viewfinder). It ignores the extreme edges and corners.

When to use it: When the subject is centered and surrounded by significantly brighter or darker areas (e.g., a person standing in a doorway or moderate backlighting). It provides more control than Evaluative without being too narrow.

3. Spot Metering (Icon: A tiny dot/circle in the center)

Measures a very small, critical area (about 1.5% of the viewfinder). Crucially, this meter is linked to the active autofocus point, meaning you can move the spot meter around the scene.

When to use it: For maximum precision in extremely high-contrast situations. Use it to meter off a specific tone you want to render as middle gray, such as a face in deep shadow or a critical highlight in a wedding dress. This requires experience but offers the most control.

4. Center-Weighted Average Metering (Icon: A square outline with a dot in the center)

Measures the entire scene but gives the heaviest weighting (priority) to the center area. Unlike Evaluative, it does not prioritize the active AF point.

When to use it: Often favored by traditional photographers or those shooting in controlled studio environments where the light is consistent and the main subject is centered.

White Balance: Achieving Accurate Color

White Balance (WB) adjusts the camera's color rendering to compensate for the color temperature of the light source, ensuring that colors appear natural and accurate. While shooting RAW allows for WB adjustments later, getting it right in-camera ensures accurate previews and faster workflow.

Step-by-Step: Setting White Balance

1. Press the WB button (located on the top control panel near the ISO button) or access the setting via the Quick Control Screen.

2. Use the Main Dial to cycle through the available settings.

Using Auto WB and Presets

Auto White Balance (AWB): The camera attempts to detect the light source and neutralize the color cast. Use AWB for general shooting or when light conditions change frequently. It is highly effective but sometimes inaccurate under mixed lighting.

White Balance Presets: These are calibrated for specific color temperatures (measured in Kelvin):

- Daylight: Bright, midday sun.
- Shade: Very blue light (high Kelvin).
- Cloudy: Slightly blue light.
- Tungsten: Very orange/yellow light (low Kelvin), common indoors.
- Fluorescent: Compensates for common green casts.
- Flash: Optimized for the cooler color of electronic flash units.

Setting a Custom White Balance Reading

Custom WB is the most reliable method for achieving perfect color accuracy under unique or difficult lighting (e.g., theatrical lighting, unusual bulbs, or indoor/outdoor mixes).

1. Photograph a Reference Target: Find a neutral subject a standard gray card, a white sheet of paper, or a white balance calibration tool. Place it where your subject will be, filling the frame in the light you are shooting under.

2. Access the Menu: Navigate to the Red Shooting Menu tab.

3. Select Custom White Balance (C.Fn III: Other, option 1).

4. Choose the Reference Image: Select the image you just took of the gray card/neutral target. Press SET. The camera confirms that the WB data has been imported.

5. Activate Custom WB: Return to the main White Balance setting screen (using the WB button).

Select the Custom WB icon (which looks like a square with triangles and the Kelvin degree measurement). Your camera is now precisely calibrated to that specific lighting condition.

High ISO Performance, Noise Control, and Low-Light Settings

The Canon EOS 5D Mark IV offers exceptional noise performance for a DSLR, allowing photographers to confidently shoot in demanding low-light conditions. However, achieving clean images requires proactive management of ISO settings and in-camera noise reduction. By setting intelligent limits, you establish the guardrails that prevent your camera from pushing the sensitivity too far and degrading image quality.

Setting ISO Range Limits

When shooting in Manual (M) mode or any semi-automatic mode (Av, Tv) using Auto ISO, the camera must be told the acceptable boundaries for sensitivity.

1. Access ISO Settings: Press the Menu button and navigate to the first Red Shooting Settings tab (Camera icon). Select ISO speed settings.

2. Set ISO Speed Range: Select ISO speed range. Here you will define the highest and lowest ISO the camera will ever select.

Minimum: Typically set this to ISO 100, the camera's native base sensitivity, which provides the cleanest image quality.

Maximum: A safe and practical upper limit for the 5D Mark IV is typically ISO 6400. While the camera can reach much higher (up to H2: ISO 102400), quality drops significantly above this point.

For professional work, consider limiting the maximum to 12800 if heavy noise reduction will be applied in post-processing.

Configuring Auto ISO Behavior

Auto ISO is a powerful tool, especially in Aperture Priority (Av) or Shutter Priority (Tv) modes, as it automatically adjusts the exposure triangle while you control two variables. However, in Av mode, you must ensure the camera does not select a shutter speed so low that it introduces motion blur.

1. Access Auto ISO Control: In the ISO speed settings menu (Red Tab 1), select Auto ISO minimum shutter speed.

2. Set Minimum Shutter Speed:

Auto (Recommended for general use): The camera intelligently sets the minimum shutter speed based on the focal length of the lens attached (the inverse rulee.g., 1/100s for a 100mm lens).

Manual Minimum: For action in low light (e.g., street photography or dim sports), you may need a higher minimum speed. Select Manual and set a floor, such as 1/125th of a second.

The camera will prioritize maintaining this shutter speed, only raising the ISO or opening the aperture (if in Tv mode) to compensate.

Managing High ISO Noise Reduction

The 5D Mark IV applies noise reduction (NR) to all recorded JPEG files. While the noise reduction is subtle in RAW files, it is crucial to understand its impact, particularly if you shoot JPEG or RAW + JPEG.

1. Locate Noise Reduction Settings: Press the Menu button and navigate to the Orange Custom Functions tab (C.Fn). Select C.Fn II: Image.

2. Adjust High ISO Speed NR: Enter this setting to choose the reduction strength:

Standard: A good balance for everyday JPEG shooting.

Low: Ideal for JPEGs where you want to retain maximum texture and detail but still suppress color noise.

Disable: Only recommended if you shoot exclusively in RAW and plan to apply all noise reduction externally using advanced software.

High: Use sparingly. While it provides the cleanest JPEGs, it often leads to a noticeable loss of fine detail and texture (the "smearing" effect).

The Trade-Off: Noise vs. Detail

The fundamental principle of low-light photography is the trade-off between reducing visible digital noise (grain) and preserving fine image detail.

In-Camera NR (High setting): Aggressively reduces noise, but often sacrifices details like hair texture, fabric weave, and fine landscape elements, making the image look softer or "painted."

RAW Control: Shooting RAW provides the greatest flexibility. You can allow the noise to exist in the captured file (by setting in-camera NR to Low or Disable) and use advanced, non-destructive noise reduction tools in your editing software, which typically offer better results than the camera's built-in processing.

For optimal low-light results with the 5D Mark IV: Set your maximum ISO range to 6400 or 12800, ensure your Auto ISO minimum shutter speed is adequate to prevent motion blur, and keep the High ISO Noise Reduction set to Low or Standard if shooting JPEG, or Disable if you plan on rigorous RAW post-processing.

CHAPTER 6

RAW, JPEG, and In-Camera Image Control

Up until this point, we have focused on technical proficiency: mastering exposure, focus, and achieving consistent light. Now, w shift our attention to efficiency and image management, ensuring that the precision we capture in the field translates seamlessly into the editing suite. Your workflow does not begin when you open your editing software; it begins the instant you select your file format on the Canon EOS 5D Mark IV.

The choice between shooting RAW, JPEG, or both simultaneously is perhaps the most fundamental decision affecting storage, flexibility, and post-processing time. A RAW file offers maximum data and control, while a JPEG provides instant usability and a smaller footprint.

Understanding the technical differences between these formats and deliberately choosing the correct option for your specific assignment is the first step toward building an efficient, professional workflow.

This chapter will serve as your comprehensive guide to setting image quality. I will demystify the core file formats and provide decisive guidance on when to choose one over the other.

Crucially, we will also explore the powerful internal processing tools available in the 5D Mark IVspecifically Picture Styles and Lens Aberration Correction. These features allow you to fine-tune the look and feel of your images (especially JPEGs) right at the moment of capture, helping you achieve a final product faster.

By mastering the settings detailed here, you will eliminate guesswork, reduce time spent on repetitive edits, and ensure that the digital files you create are perfectly optimized for your desired output, whether that means extensive retouching or immediate client delivery.

Choosing RAW or JPEG Based on Workflow and Storage

Choosing the correct file format is one of the most fundamental decisions you make on the 5D Mark IV, as it dictates your editing flexibility, storage needs, and overall workflow speed. The choice between RAW and JPEG is a trade-off between absolute quality control and operational efficiency.

RAW files, often called digital negatives, are the unprocessed, uncompressed data recorded directly from the camera sensor. They contain maximum dynamic range and color information, meaning they offer tremendous flexibility for adjustment in post-processing.

JPEG files, on the other hand, are compressed files that have already been processed by the camera's internal computer, applying settings like Picture Style, sharpening, and White Balance. They are ready to use immediately but sacrifice editing latitude.

RAW vs. JPEG: A Side-by-Side Comparison

RAW Files (e.g., RAW, M-RAW, S-RAW)

Pros

Maximum Flexibility: Unrivaled ability to recover detail in shadows or highlights. White Balance and exposure can be drastically changed without damaging the image.

14-Bit Color Depth: Records far more color information (over 16,000 tones per channel), resulting in smoother gradients.

Non-Destructive: Original sensor data is always preserved, allowing unlimited editing revisions.

Cons

Large File Size: Requires significantly more storage space on cards and hard drives (30-50MB+).

Mandatory Workflow: Requires post-processing software (Lightroom, Capture One, etc.) and time to process before delivery.

Slower Burst Shooting: Large files slow the camera's buffer, limiting the maximum number of continuous shots.

JPEG Files (e.g., L, M, S1)

Pros

Immediate Use: Files are ready to print, upload, or share right after capture.

Small File Size: Saves substantial storage space (5-10MB) and allows for quicker transfer times.

Faster Workflow: No mandatory post-processing required for basic use.

Maximum Burst Shooting: Enables the fastest possible continuous shooting rate because the files are small and compressed.

Cons

Limited Editing: Significant changes to exposure or White Balance quickly degrade image quality dueizing 8-bit color depth.

Lossy Compression: Details and tones are discarded during the compression process.

Fixed Color/Style: White Balance and Picture Style choices are baked into the file at the moment of capture.

Selecting Image Quality Settings (RAW, JPEG, or Both)

The 5D Mark IV allows you to select the file type and size independently, or combine them. Canon also provides medium (M-RAW) and small (S-RAW) versions of the RAW file, which offer slightly reduced resolution and size while maintaining the flexibility of the RAW format.

Step 1: Access the Menu

Press the MENU button on the back of the camera.

Step 2: Navigate to Image Quality

Use the joystick or Quick Control Dial to navigate to the first Red Shooting Menu tab (Shooting Menu 1).

Select "Image quality."

Step 3: Select File Type and Size

On the Image Quality screen, you will see columns for RAW, M-RAW, S-RAW, and a list of JPEG sizes (L, M, S1, S2, S3).

RAW Options: Use the Main Dial (top right) to scroll through the RAW options (RAW, M-RAW, S-RAW). Choose the desired size. Note that RAW is 30.4 megapixels, M-RAW is 16.9MP, and S-RAW is 7.6MP.

JPEG Options: Use the Quick Control Dial (back) to scroll through the JPEG options (L for Large/Highest Quality, down to S3 for Small/Lower Quality).

To select a combination, such as RAW + L (Large JPEG), use the dials until the desired file types are highlighted. Press SET to confirm.

Workflow Tip: For professional work or critical creative projects (portraits, landscapes, weddings), select the highest quality setting: RAW.

For documentation, press releases, or situations where rapid delivery is more important than minute detail, choose L (Large JPEG).

Simultaneous Recording: RAW + JPEG

The 5D Mark IV allows you to record both a RAW file and a corresponding JPEG file simultaneously for every shot. This is especially useful for hybrid workflows where editing flexibility is needed, but an immediate proof or preview file must also be available.

How to Utilize RAW + JPEG:

In the "Image quality" menu, select both a RAW setting (e.g., RAW) and a JPEG setting (e.g., L). When you take a picture, the camera writes two distinct files to your memory card(s).

Practical Application: Many wedding and event photographers use this feature. The JPEG provides a quickly accessible proof image for clients or social media previews, while the accompanying RAW file ensures that they have maximum data available later for detailed retouching and final prints.

Warning: When using RAW + JPEG, the storage space used is essentially double, and the camera's buffer fills up faster than if shooting only RAW or only JPEG. Ensure you are using fast memory cards (CF or SD) rated for high-speed transfer to maintain performance.

Picture Styles, Lens Corrections, and Image Optimization

Picture Styles and in-camera image optimization are powerful tools for achieving consistent results. Picture Styles dictate how the camera processes color, contrast, and sharpness, affecting JPEG files directly and providing a preview for RAW files. Enabling lens corrections ensures your images are free of common optical flaws before they even reach your computer.

Choosing and Customizing Picture Styles

Picture Styles are essentially pre-set chemical recipes for your digital images. They allow you to apply specific looks such as punchy contrast (Standard) or soft, flat color (Neutral)at the time of capture.

Step 1: Accessing Picture Styles

1. Press the MENU button.

2. Navigate to the first red Shooting Menu tab (Shooting Menu 3).

3. Select Picture Style.

Step 2: Selecting a Base Style

You will see a list of pre-set styles. Choose the one that best suits your needs:

- Standard: Default, highly versatile style with slightly boosted saturation and contrast. Best for general use.
- Portrait: Softer contrast and slightly less saturated colors, optimized for skin tones.
- Landscape: Stronger contrast, higher saturation, and increased sharpness, especially for blues and greens.
- Neutral: Minimal sharpening, saturation, and contrast. Ideal for RAW shooters who want the flattest possible file for maximum editing flexibility.
- Faithful: Designed to render colors exactly as they are viewed in natural light. Minimal processing.

Step 3: Customizing a Style (User Defined)

If you wish to fine-tune a style, you can adjust its parameters and save it to a User Defined slot (User Def 1, 2, or 3).

1. Highlight your desired base Picture Style (or one of the User Def slots).

2. Press the INFO button (or press SET, depending on the current firmware version) to enter the detail settings.

3. Adjust the following parameters:

Sharpness: Controls the crispness of edges. The 5D Mark IV allows adjustment of Strength, Fineness, and Threshold.

Contrast: Controls the difference between light and dark areas.

Saturation: Controls the intensity of the colors.

Color Tone: Controls the warmth or coolness of the image.

4. Press MENU to exit and save your customized style to the selected User Def slot.

Picture Styles and File Formats

It is crucial to understand how Picture Styles affect your file format:

JPEG: The selected Picture Style is permanently applied to the image. If you shoot Standard, the final JPEG will have the Standard look.

RAW: The Picture Style acts only as a preview. It influences what you see on the camera's LCD screen and histogram, but the raw image data remains untouched.

If you open the RAW file in Canon’s Digital Photo Professional (DPP) software, the Picture Style is recognized and applied, but if you use third-party software like Adobe Lightroom, the image will appear flat (closer to Neutral), requiring manual application of the style. RAW shooters often prefer Neutral or Faithful for the most unadulterated starting point.

In-Camera Lens Aberration Correction

Lenses, even high-end ones, exhibit optical flaws that can be automatically corrected by the 5D Mark IV using built-in software profiles. Enabling these features improves image quality and saves time during post-processing.

Step 1: Locating Corrections

1. Press the MENU button.

2. Navigate to the first red Shooting Menu tab (Shooting Menu 3).

3. Select 'Lens aberration correction'.

Step 2: Enabling Peripheral Illumination Correction

Peripheral illumination correction addresses vignetting the darkening of the image corners, often visible when shooting with wide apertures.

1. Select 'Peripheral illum. correction'.

2. Choose 'Enable'.

Why Enable It? Vignetting can be distracting, especially in skies or plain backgrounds. The camera automatically brightens the corners based on the specific lens attached and the aperture used, resulting in a more uniform exposure across the frame.

Step 3: Enabling Chromatic Aberration Correction

Chromatic aberration correction targets color fringing the purple, blue, or green halos that appear around high-contrast edges (e.g., tree branches against a bright sky).

1. Select 'Chromatic aberr. correction'.

2. Choose 'Enable'.

Why Enable It? Chromatic aberration is a common lens defect that is difficult to remove manually in bulk. The 5D Mark IV automatically detects and subtracts these unwanted color shifts, leading to visibly cleaner, sharper edges.

Note on Lens Data: For these corrections to work, the camera must have profile data for the lens being used.

The 5D Mark IV is pre-loaded with data for many popular Canon EF lenses, and can automatically download profiles for newer lenses when connected via Wi-Fi or Canon utility software.

If a correction is shown as 'Data available for selected lens', the correction is active and running.

CHAPTER 7

Customizing the Camera to Work Like You Do

The Canon EOS 5D Mark IV is a powerful photographic instrument, but simply knowing where the buttons are located is not enough to truly master it. Mastery comes when the camera ceases to feel like a separate piece of technology and instead becomes a seamless extension of your creative visionan extension of your eye and your hand.

Out of the box, the 5D Mark IV is configured for generalized use. For professional or advanced shooting, this often means constantly interrupting your creative flow to dive into deep menu structures to adjust settings like metering, AF tracking sensitivity, or button assignments. These delays lead to missed moments and frustration.

This chapter is dedicated entirely to eliminating those workflow interruptions. We will transform your 5D Mark IV from a standard tool into a highly personalized shooting machine, optimized precisely for your unique style, whether you shoot fast-paced weddings, methodical landscapes, or urgent photojournalism.

We will focus on implementing three critical efficiency measures:

1. Strategic use of Custom Functions (C.Fn) to redefine what various buttons and dials do, placing essential controls immediately under your fingers.

2. Creating and managing the My Menu system, ensuring your most frequently adjusted settings are never more than a single press away.

3. Leveraging the Custom Shooting Modes (C1, C2, and C3) to save and instantly recall complete camera setups for specific scenarios (e.g., one setting for fast action, another for studio portraiture).

By the end of this section, you will stop thinking about where a setting is and start focusing purely on the act of creation. This is where efficiency meets artistry, guaranteeing that your camera is always ready to capture the shot exactly when you need it.

Custom Functions That Dramatically Improve Speed and Control

The true power of the Canon EOS 5D Mark IV lies not in its default settings, but in its deep customization potential via the Custom Functions (C.Fn) menu. By reassigning controls, you can eliminate the need to dive into the main menu system, making the camera an instantaneous extension of your creative decisions.

Access the Custom Functions menu by navigating to the orange wrench tab, selecting the C.Fn option, and drilling down into the numbered categories (I, II, III, IV).

Optimizing the Custom Controls (C.Fn III-4)

The most significant customization is mapping specific controls to functions you use constantly. This is done through C.Fn III: Operation/Other > Custom Controls (C.Fn III-4). This menu allows you to specify the function of nearly every critical button on the camera body.

1. Reassigning the SET Button for AF Area Selection

The SET button, located in the center of the Quick Control Dial, is often underutilized in its default setting. Reassigning it provides immediate access to critical focus tools.

Step-by-Step Setup:

1. Navigate to C.Fn III: Operation/Other > Custom Controls (C.Fn III-4).

2. Select the option labeled SET button.

3. Change the assignment from its default (often 'Menu Display') to Select AF Area.

Real-World Benefit: Instead of pressing the AF Point Selection button and then rotating dials to switch between Single-Point AF, Zone AF, or automatic selection, you can now simply press the SET button. This allows you to rapidly change the focus grouping type without taking your eye from the viewfinder, essential for subjects that change movement patterns quickly.

2. Controlling the Direction of Dials (C.Fn IV-1)

If you have transitioned from a different camera system (even another Canon series), you may find the direction in which the Main Dial (top right) or Quick Control Dial (rear) adjusts exposure values counter-intuitive. Custom Function IV-1 allows you to standardize the direction for efficiency.

Step-by-Step Setup:

1. Navigate to C.Fn IV: Operation/Other > Dials (C.Fn IV-1).

2. You will see options for Main Dial (top) and Quick Control Dial (rear).

3. Select the dial you wish to change (e.g., Quick Control Dial).

4. Change the direction setting (Normal or Reversed).

Real-World Benefit: Ensuring that rotating the dial right always increases the value (faster shutter speed, wider aperture, higher ISO) or left always decreases it eliminates costly hesitation and errors when working quickly in Manual or semi-automatic modes.

3. Assigning the Depth of Field Preview Button

The Depth of Field (DoF) Preview button, located low on the camera front near the lens mount, is perfectly positioned for the ring finger and can be assigned to a more frequently needed function than just DoF preview.

Recommended Setup: Metering Mode Selection

1. Navigate to C.Fn III: Operation/Other > Custom Controls (C.Fn III-4).

2. Select Depth-of-Field preview button.

3. Assign this button to Metering Mode.

Real-World Benefit: When shooting backlit subjects, you often need to switch instantly from Evaluative (all-encompassing) metering to Spot metering (focusing only on the subject). Using the DoF button bypasses the need to use the dedicated metering button on the back, keeping your finger ready to press the shutter.

4. Enabling Register/Recall Shooting Function (C.Fn III-4)

For photographers who switch frequently between two very specific, pre-set configurations (e.g., a landscape setup versus an immediate wildlife burst setup), assigning a button to instantly recall a registered set of settings is invaluable.

Recommended Setup: Assigning to the AF-ON Button

While the AF-ON button is typically used for Back-Button Focus, if you prefer to retain AF on the shutter, you can use the AF-ON button to instantly switch modes.

1. Navigate to C.Fn III: Operation/Other > Custom Controls (C.Fn III-4).

2. Select AF-ON button.

3. Assign this button to Register/recall shooting func. (Make sure you have registered your desired settings first by navigating to the same menu and using the Register setting option).

Real-World Benefit: Imagine shooting portraits (low burst, One-Shot AF) and suddenly needing to capture a fleeting action shot (high burst, AI Servo, fast shutter). Pressing the assigned AF-ON button instantly loads the registered action profile, saving valuable seconds otherwise spent manually changing three or four settings.

5. Optimizing Button Function Delays

While the 5D Mark IV does not have a general setting to adjust button delay sensitivity, its responsiveness is governed by C.Fn III-4. For specialized functions, you can configure how long a button must be held down to activate.

Example: If you assign a critical function (like changing AF Case) to a button like the M-Fn, ensuring its action is instantaneous is crucial.

By ensuring the function is set to be triggered by a single press rather than a 'hold and adjust' action, you maximize speed. Always test your custom assignment in C.Fn III-4 to ensure it triggers the function you expect immediately upon pressing, thereby minimizing operational delay.

My Menu and Custom Shooting Modes (C1, C2, C3)

The EOS 5D Mark IV offers two powerful tools designed to eliminate time spent digging through menus, allowing you to react instantly to changing environments. Mastering the My Menu tab and the Custom Shooting Modes (C1, C2, C3) will transform your workflow efficiency.

My Menu: Your Personalized Menu Tab

The My Menu tab is represented by the Star icon () at the end of the main menu bar. It allows you to register up to six tabs, each holding up to six of your most-used menu items, regardless of where those items reside in the main menu system.

Creating and Organizing My Menu

Step 1: Access and Add a Tab

1. Press the MENU button.

2. Navigate to the last tab group, marked with a black star ().

3. Select 'My Menu settings' and then choose 'Register a My Menu tab'. (The camera will usually prompt you to register the first tab automatically.)

Step 2: Register Menu Items

1. Within the My Menu settings, select 'Register items'.

2. You will see a list of every single setting available in the camera's menu system. Scroll through the tabs (Shoot, AF, Playback, Setup, Custom Functions) to find the settings you use most often.

3. Common items to register include: Format card, Custom White Balance, Flicker detection, High ISO Noise Reduction, and the various Autofocus Case settings.

4. Select the item and press SET to confirm registration.

Step 3: Organize and Prioritize

1. After registering items, return to 'My Menu settings'.

2. Use the 'Sort' option to rearrange items within the tab, placing the most critical ones at the top.

3. Use 'Delete items' to remove settings you no longer need quick access to.

4. To maximize efficiency, select 'Display from My Menu tab' (found within My Menu settings). This ensures that every time you press the MENU button, the customized My Menu is the first screen you see, saving you crucial seconds.

Custom Shooting Modes (C1, C2, C3)

The C1, C2, and C3 positions on the Mode Dial are essential for photographers working in varied environments (e.g., weddings, journalism, or wildlife). These modes allow you to save and instantly recall a complete camera configuration including exposure settings, metering, AF mode, AF Case, drive mode, image quality (RAW/JPEG), and even custom function settings.

Saving Your Custom Configurations

Step 1: Set Up the Camera

1. Turn the Mode Dial to Av, Tv, or M.

2. Configure the camera exactly as you would want it for a specific scenario. For example, for wildlife:

a. Exposure Mode: Tv (Shutter Priority)

b. Shutter Speed: 1/1000 sec

c. ISO: Auto ISO (with limits set)

d. AF Mode: AI Servo

e. AF Case: Case 2 (Continue tracking ignoring possible obstacles)

f. Drive Mode: High-speed continuous

Step 2: Access the Registration Menu

1. Press the MENU button and navigate to the Setup Tab 5 (Wrench Icon).

2. Select 'Custom shooting mode (C1-C3)'.

3. Select 'Register settings'.

Step 3: Register and Save

1. On the registration screen, choose the location you want to save the settings to (C1, C2, or C3). Use C1 for your most common configuration.

2. The camera displays a summary of the current settings being saved. Press OK to confirm.

Using and Protecting Custom Modes

Once registered, you can instantly switch to that complex configuration by turning the Mode Dial to C1, C2, or C3. This is far faster than manually adjusting multiple settings on the fly.

Preventing Accidental Overwrites

When you shoot in C1, C2, or C3, the camera allows you to make temporary adjustments (e.g., changing the shutter speed or ISO). If you turn the dial away and then return, the camera will revert to the original saved settings.

However, if you want the camera to permanently save your temporary changes every time you power down, you must adjust the 'Auto update set' option, found under Setup Tab 5 > 'Custom shooting mode (C1-C3)'.

Recommendation: For professional use, set 'Auto update set' to Disable. This ensures that the saved C1 configuration remains pristine and unchanged, giving you a reliable, known baseline every time you select the mode. If you need to save an updated configuration, repeat the 'Register settings' process.

CHAPTER 8

Lenses, Depth, and Stabilization in Practice

You have spent the preceding chapters mastering the engine of the Canon EOS 5D Mark IVits exposure controls, its customization options, and its sophisticated autofocus system.

However, even the most powerful camera body is useless without the correct lens attached, as the lens is the eye of your system. It is the optical element that dictates two fundamental qualities of your photograph: perspective and sharpness.

Many photographers treat their glass as an afterthought, but your choice of lens, and your mastery of the optical principles it governs, is what separates a good image from a superior one. The lens is responsible for the aesthetic 'look' of your images, determining how shallow your depth of field can be, and how distortion or perspective affects your composition.

This chapter shifts our focus from the internal settings of the 5D Mark IV to the external tools that interact directly with the light. We will guide you through choosing the right EF lens for your specific photographic style, explaining Canon's crucial lens terminology and offering actionable advice on selecting focal lengths for portraiture, landscape, and action.

Crucially, we will focus on practical application. You will learn how to manually control depth of field using the preview function, and how to maximize sharpness across entire scenes without relying on complex calculations.

Finally, we will cover the necessity of image stabilization (IS), providing step-by-step instructions on when and how to engage the appropriate IS mode on your lenses to ensure consistently sharp results, even in low light or high-movement scenarios. Mastery of optics is the final, essential step toward confident image creation.

Choosing the Right EF Lens for Your Shooting Style

The Canon EOS 5D Mark IV uses the extensive EF lens system, offering a vast array of choices that often overwhelm new users. It is crucial to remember that the lens defines the look, feel, sharpness, and overall quality of your image far more than the camera body does. Choosing the right optics means aligning the lens characteristics focal length and aperture with your specific creative goals.

Decoding Canon Lens Designations

Understanding the acronyms on a Canon lens barrel is the first step toward making an informed purchase:

L Series (Luxury)

Designated by a red ring around the front barrel, 'L' lenses are Canon's professional-grade optics. They feature superior glass elements, enhanced weather sealing, and robust construction, delivering the sharpest image quality possible. If your photography is professional or mission-critical, prioritize L-series glass.

USM (Ultrasonic Motor)

This indicates a high-speed, highly precise, and extremely quiet autofocus motor. USM is essential for tracking fast-moving subjects (wildlife, sports) and for rapid focus acquisition in dynamic shooting environments. Many USM lenses also feature full-time manual focus override.

IS (Image Stabilization)

Image Stabilization uses internal gyroscope sensors to detect and counteract subtle camera movement. This is critical when shooting handheld at slower shutter speeds, especially with telephoto lenses. IS is typically marked by different modes (Mode 1 for still subjects, Mode 2 for panning).

STM (Stepping Motor)

While less common on high-end EF lenses than USM, the STM designation signifies a motor optimized for extremely smooth and silent focus transitions, making it ideal for video recording and Live View shooting where noise is a concern.

Focal Length and Perspective

The focal length is perhaps the most important choice, as it dictates the composition and the sense of space in your final image:

Wide Angle (16mm to 35mm)

These lenses push the subject away, exaggerating perspective and making spaces feel expansive. They are ideal for landscapes, architecture, and interior shots. Be mindful of distortion at the extreme wide end, which can be corrected in-camera or in post-processing.

Standard/Normal (35mm to 85mm)

This range provides a perspective most similar to the human eye, resulting in natural-looking, undistorted images.

The 50mm lens is often called a "nifty fifty" for its versatility, speed, and sharp image quality, making it excellent for street photography and general purpose shooting. The 85mm begins to offer compression, ideal for tighter portraiture.

Telephoto (100mm and up)

Telephoto lenses compress the distance between the foreground and background, making elements appear closer together. This is highly effective for isolating a subject, blurring the background (achieving subject isolation), and capturing distant subjects like wildlife or sports action. They often require Image Stabilization or a fast shutter speed to mitigate camera shake.

Recommended Lenses by Genre

To maximize the 5D Mark IV's potential, focus on fast, sharp glass tailored to your primary work.

1. Portrait Photography

Goal: Shallow depth of field, flattering subject compression, and sharpness.

Recommendations:

85mm f/1.4L or 85mm f/1.8: The quintessential portrait lens. It provides outstanding compression and beautiful bokeh, cleanly separating the subject from the background.

135mm f/2L: A longer option offering even greater isolation and exceptionally creamy background blur.

2. Landscape and Architecture

Goal: Maximum sharpness corner-to-corner, wide field of view, and deep depth of field.

Recommendations:

16-35mm f/4L IS USM: Provides excellent wide coverage and includes IS, helpful when composing tripod-free. The f/4 aperture keeps costs down while maintaining excellent sharpness.

24-70mm f/2.8L II USM: A highly versatile mid-range zoom, ideal when versatility is needed over extreme wide-angle reach.

3. Wedding and Event Photography (The Professional Trinity)

Goal: Versatility, speed (fast aperture), reliability, and low-light performance.

Recommendations:

24-70mm f/2.8L II USM: The workhorse. This covers essential reception, ceremony, and preparation settings. The constant f/2.8 aperture is crucial for low light.

70-200mm f/2.8L IS USM: Necessary for isolating the couple during the ceremony and for capturing detail from a distance. The IS is invaluable here.

35mm f/1.4L or 50mm f/1.2L: A fast prime lens is required for extremely dark environments or when trying to achieve maximum separation and a distinct documentary style.

Depth of Field Control and Image Stabilization Techniques

The Depth of Field Preview button is one of the most underutilized controls on the 5D Mark IV, yet it provides immediate visual feedback on the sharpness of your image at a given aperture. Unlike the standard viewfinder view, which always keeps the aperture wide open for maximum brightness, the DoF Preview temporarily stops the lens down to the exact aperture setting you have chosen.

Using the Depth of Field Preview Button

1. Set Your Aperture: Ensure the camera is set to Av (Aperture Priority) or M (Manual) mode, and dial in the desired f/stop (e.g., f/4 for a portrait, f/16 for a landscape).

2. Locate the Button: The DoF Preview button is typically located on the lower front side of the camera, near the lens release button.

3. Press and Hold: Look through the optical viewfinder (OVF) and press and hold this button.

4. Observe the Change: The viewfinder image will immediately become darker, reflecting the reduced light passing through the lens. Critically, you will now see exactly which parts of your frame are sharp and which are blurred.

5. Practical Use: Use this feature, especially when shooting wide open (e.g., f/2.8) for portraits, to confirm that essential features like the subject's eyes remain in focus, or when shooting landscapes at small apertures (f/11) to check that the foreground is adequately sharp.

Achieving Maximum Landscape Sharpness with Hyperfocal Distance

Hyperfocal distance is a concept used to establish the maximum depth of field possible for a given focal length and aperture setting, resulting in objects sharp from a close foreground point all the way to infinity. While the complex math is unnecessary for modern digital photography, the principle remains crucial for landscapes.

The simple, actionable rule for achieving near-to-far sharpness without guessing is:

1. Use a Wide Lens: Begin with a wide-angle lens (e.g., 16mm to 35mm).

2. Choose a Narrow Aperture: Select an aperture between f/11 and f/16. While f/22 offers more depth, it often introduces visible softness due to diffraction.

3. Focus Point Selection: Instead of focusing directly on the nearest object or infinity, select a focus point that is approximately one-third of the way into your scene. For example, if your foreground object is 3 feet away, focus on something about 5 or 6 feet away.

4. Confirm with Live View: Switch to Live View and zoom in (using the Magnify button) on both the closest sharp object and the furthest object (the horizon). Both should appear equally sharp, confirming the use of hyperfocal distance.

Mastering Lens-Based Image Stabilization (IS)

Canon lenses equipped with Image Stabilization (IS) feature a physical switch offering different stabilization modes. Understanding when to use each mode is vital for ensuring handheld sharpness. Always remember that IS is a mechanism to counteract camera shake, not subject movement, and should generally be turned OFF when the camera is mounted on a sturdy tripod.

IS Mode 1 (Standard)

Mode 1 is the default and most common setting. It provides stabilization across both the horizontal and vertical axes.

Use Case: Ideal for stationary subjects, general handheld photography (portraits, landscapes, street photography), and shots taken while standing still or walking slowly.

IS Mode 2 (Panning)

Mode 2 activates stabilization only on the axis perpendicular to your movement. If you are tracking a moving object horizontally, Mode 2 will stabilize the vertical movement (up and down shake) but allow the horizontal movement (the pan) to remain free.

Use Case: Essential for tracking moving subjects like race cars, birds in flight, or cyclists. Hold the camera steady and move smoothly along the path of the subject.

IS Mode 3 (Exposure Only)

Mode 3 is the most advanced and often preferred by action photographers. The stabilization system is kept 'on hold' and only activates the instant the shutter button is fully pressed, during the actual exposure. This prevents potential issues where the IS mechanism tries to stabilize movement before the shot, which can sometimes interfere with quick framing adjustments.

Use Case: Excellent for erratic movement, sports, and rapid burst shooting where the photographer is framing shots very quickly.

CHAPTER 9

Shooting Confident Video with the 5D Mark IV

The Canon EOS 5D Mark IV is not just an iconic still camera; it is also a cinematic powerhouse. Since its inception, the 5D line has fundamentally changed the landscape of independent filmmaking, and the Mark IV continues that legacy with high-resolution 4K capabilities and revolutionary Dual Pixel CMOS AF.

For many photographers, however, the world of motion capture with its demands for consistent frame rates, controlled audio, and seamless focus tracking can feel entirely separate from still photography.

The transition from capturing a single perfect moment to recording 24 or 30 moments per second requires adjusting your mindset and mastering a completely different set of controls.

This chapter is your bridge. We will treat the 5D Mark IV's Movie Mode as a distinct, specialized tool and walk through its configuration step-by-step. Our focus is eliminating the confusion surrounding video settings so you can achieve high-quality, usable footage immediately.

I will demystify the choices between 4K and 1080p, explain why frame rate is more than just speed, and show you exactly how to set your camera's exposure controls for a true cinematic look.

You will learn how to transition confidently from traditional viewfinder shooting to utilizing the Live View screen and how to manage the crucial component of video production that stills photographers often overlook: clean, professional audio.

By the end of this guide, the video switch on your camera will become an active and essential part of your creative toolkit.

Video Settings Explained: Resolution, Frame Rates, and Profiles

Entering the video environment requires navigating to the Movie Shooting menu (indicated by a red camera icon). Before hitting the record button, three primary settings must be configured for optimal video output: Movie Recording Size (Resolution and Frame Rate) and Compression.

Movie Recording Size (Resolution and Frame Rate)

This critical menu selection determines both the physical dimensions of the video (resolution) and the speed at which frames are captured (frame rate).

Step 1: Navigate to the Movie Shooting Menu

Press the Menu button, navigate to the Red Menu Tabs, and select the appropriate tab (typically the second or third red tab) to find Movie rec. size.

Step 2: Select Resolution (4K vs. 1080p)

The Canon 5D Mark IV offers two main resolution standards:

4K (4096 x 2160 DCI): This is the highest resolution option, delivering maximum detail and flexibility for cropping in post-production.

Caveat: When shooting 4K on the 5D Mark IV, the camera imposes a significant 1.64x crop factor. This means your effective focal length is multiplied, making wide-angle shooting challenging. For instance, a 24mm lens behaves like a 40mm lens in 4K mode.

Full HD (1920 x 1080): This is the most versatile and commonly used setting. It produces high-quality video without any sensor cropping (full frame) and results in smaller file sizes that require less powerful computers for editing.

Step 3: Choose Frame Rate (p stands for Progressive scan)

The choice of frame rate dictates the visual appearance of motion.

24p (23.98 fps): The international standard for cinema and narrative film. Shooting at 24p provides a subtle motion blur, often described as the "cinematic look." Use this setting when you want your footage to look polished and film-like.

30p (29.97 fps): The standard for North American television, news, and general content. This frame rate provides a slightly sharper, less blurred look than 24p and is ideal for fast-paced content where a cinematic feel is not the priority.

60p (59.94 fps): Used almost exclusively for slow-motion recording. To achieve smooth slow motion, you record at 60p and then play the footage back at 30p or 24p in your editing software. This effectively halves the speed of the action, which is perfect for dramatic emphasis, sports, or nature videography.

Note: Higher frame rates (like 60p) are often only available when selecting Full HD (1080p) resolution.

Compression Options (ALL-I vs. IPB)

Compression determines how the camera processes and stores the video data on the memory card. This setting is often tied directly to the Movie rec. size selection.

IPB (Inter-frame compression): This is the standard compression method. The camera efficiently compresses data by referencing information across multiple frames (groups of pictures).

Pros: Produces much smaller file sizes, allowing for longer recording times and easing storage demands.

Cons: Less robust for heavy editing, complex color grading, or frame-by-frame analysis, as data is discarded during compression.

ALL-I (Intra-frame compression): This advanced compression method records every frame individually, independent of the surrounding frames.

Pros: Provides the highest quality video signal for demanding post-production workflows. It is essential for keying, intensive color correction, or professional effects.

Cons: Produces extremely large files (often two to three times the size of IPB files) and requires high-speed memory cards (such as UDMA 7 CF cards) to maintain recording without interruption.

Choice: For most users, IPB offers a perfect balance of quality and efficiency. Choose ALL-I only when you know your project requires maximum flexibility in a professional editing suite.

Dual Pixel AF, Manual Focus, and Cinematic Control

The Canon EOS 5D Mark IV's most significant advancement for videographers is its revolutionary Dual Pixel CMOS AF (DPAF). This system uses phase-detection points embedded directly onto the imaging sensor, allowing for extremely smooth, precise, and fast autofocus tracking during video recording a feature critical for professional results.

Utilizing Dual Pixel AF for Smooth Video

To leverage DPAF, you must first ensure Movie Servo AF is enabled.

1. Switch the mode dial to the movie camera icon (Live View/Video mode).

2. Press the MENU button, navigate to the [Red Menu (Shooting)], and find the Movie Servo AF setting. Ensure it is set to [Enable].

3. Set the AF Method to either [Face Tracking + Tracking] (ideal for people) or [FlexiZone - Single Point] (ideal for fixed objects).

The true power of DPAF in video is the ability to customize focus transition speed:

Movie Servo AF Speed

This setting dictates how fast the camera racks focus from one point to another.

Location: [Red Menu (Shooting)] > Movie Servo AF speed.

Cinematic Look: Set the speed slower (towards the minus side, e.g., -4 or -5). This provides a gentle, professional focus pull, ensuring the viewer's eye follows the subject naturally.

Fast Action/Documentary: Set the speed faster (towards the plus side). This provides immediate focus locking, necessary when subjects move quickly or erratically.

Touchscreen Tracking

Once DPAF is enabled, the easiest way to initiate a focus pull or lock focus onto a specific subject is by using the touch screen.

Simply tap the subject on the LCD display; the camera will smoothly and continuously track that subject, even if it moves slightly within the frame. Tapping a new area on the screen will execute a smooth focus transition (rack focus) to that point at the speed you set.

Achieving Sharp Manual Focus

While DPAF is excellent, certain professional scenarios especially those requiring extremely precise focus or highly controlled, slow focus pulls demand manual focus (MF).

1. Set Lens to MF: Always switch the AF/MF switch on the lens barrel to MF.

2. Engage Live View Magnification: While in video standby mode (Live View), press the Magnify button (usually labeled with a magnifying glass icon, located near the top right of the LCD).

3. Zoom In: Repeatedly press the Magnify button to cycle through 5x and 10x magnification. This is your most crucial tool for accurate MF.

4. Adjust Focus: Adjust the focus ring on your lens until the desired point (an eye, a fabric texture, etc.) is critically sharp at 10x magnification.

5. Return to Full View: Press the Magnify button again to return to normal view before hitting record.

Cinematic Exposure Using Manual Controls

To ensure your video footage has a professional, cinematic look, you must control the shutter speed independently of the exposure, adhering to the 180-Degree Shutter Angle Rule. This rule governs motion blur, ensuring movement looks natural rather than choppy or excessively smeared.

1. Set Movie Mode to Manual: Ensure your camera is in Manual (M) mode while recording video (set via the mode dial or menu). This locks both aperture and shutter speed.

2. Apply the 180-Degree Rule: The rule states that your shutter speed should be roughly double your frame rate.

If shooting 24 frames per second (24p) for a traditional film look, set the shutter speed to 1/50 second.

If shooting 30 frames per second (30p), set the shutter speed to 1/60 second.

If shooting 60 frames per second (60p) for slow motion, set the shutter speed to 1/125 second.

3. Control Exposure with Aperture and ISO: Once the shutter speed is locked to the appropriate cinematic value, you control the brightness (exposure) using only the aperture (for depth of field) and the ISO.

4. Use ND Filters in Bright Light: If you set a slow shutter speed (like 1/50 sec) and want to use a wide aperture (like f/2.8) on a sunny day, your image will be grossly overexposed.

To compensate, you must attach Neutral Density (ND) filters to your lens. ND filters are essentially sunglasses for the camera, allowing you to maintain cinematic shutter speeds and wide apertures regardless of ambient light.

Canon
Canon
Canon
CaSask
CaSask

CHAPTER 10

Audio, Live View, and Silent Shooting

The Canon EOS 5D Mark IV is designed to excel not only in traditional still photography environments but also in highly specialized and sensitive professional settings. This chapter focuses on the operational tools that enhance your versatility and expand the scenarios in which your camera can be successfully deployed.

For any photographer serious about adding video to their skillset, mastering audio is a non-negotiable step. Clean sound elevates production quality immediately, and the 5D Mark IV offers robust controls for external microphones and monitoring that allow for artifact-free capture. I will guide you through setting up input levels and utilizing the headphone jack to ensure technical reliability.

Furthermore, professionalism often dictates discretion. Whether you are photographing a quiet wedding ceremony, a theatrical performance, or wildlife, the mechanical noise of a standard DSLR shutter can be intrusive. The techniques and settings for silent operation detailed here will ensure you can capture decisive moments without drawing attention.

Finally, we will deep dive into Live View. This mode is the gateway to precise focusing via the touchscreen, enabling you to shoot from unconventional angles and utilize the superior Dual Pixel AF system for both stills and video.

By mastering the settings in this chapter, your 5D Mark IV transforms into a truly adaptable, all-in-one imaging powerhouse, ready for any assignment that requires subtlety or advanced monitoring.

Audio Setup, Monitoring, and Clean Sound Recording

Achieving high-quality audio is just as critical as achieving sharp focus and perfect exposure in video production. While the 5D Mark IV has a built-in microphone, professional results demand an external microphone and careful configuration.

This section provides a practical guide to configuring your camera for clean, artifact-free sound capture.

Step 1: Switching to Manual Sound Recording

The first step in achieving professional audio is taking control away from the camera's automation.

1. Switch the 5D Mark IV into Movie Shooting mode using the Live View/Video toggle switch.

2. Press the Menu button.

3. Navigate to the Movie Shooting tab (Red Camera icon).

4. Select Sound Recording.

5. Set Sound Recording to Manual.

By selecting Manual, you prevent the camera from automatically adjusting the recording levels during the shoot (a process known as "Auto Gain Control" or AGC), which often leads to distracting fluctuations in volume and ‘pumping’ noise.

Step 2: Configuring Microphone Sensitivity (Recording Levels)

Once in Manual mode, you must set the appropriate sensitivity level based on your microphone choice (internal or external) and the subject's volume.

1. While still in the Sound Recording menu, look for the Rec. Level slider.

2. Observe the Level Meter displayed on the screen. This meter shows the real-time volume of the incoming sound.

3. Have your subject speak at their loudest anticipated level, or create the loudest sound you expect to record.

4. Adjust the Rec. Level slider so that the audio peaks register well within the green and yellow zones, ideally aiming for a peak between -12dB and -6dB.

5. Crucially, ensure the meter never hits the red zone (0dB). Hitting 0dB means the sound is clipping, resulting in harsh, irreversible digital distortion.

Best Practice: Always prioritize leaving adequate 'headroom' (the space between your loudest peak and 0dB) to account for unexpected spikes in volume.

Step 3: Using External Microphones

The 5D Mark IV accepts external microphones via the 3.5mm stereo mini-jack input located on the left side panel. Always use an external microphone for serious work.

1. Ensure your external microphone is correctly plugged into the MIC input jack.

2. If the microphone is powered (e.g., uses a separate battery), ensure the mic power is switched on.

3. Run a test recording and check the Level Meter. If you are using a professional microphone, you will likely need to

set the Rec. Level on the camera much lower than if you were using the built-in mic.

Step 4: Activating the Wind Filter and Attenuator

These two settings help clean up audio in challenging acoustic environments.

Wind Filter

The Wind Filter is a low-cut filter designed to remove low-frequency rumble, which is often caused by wind noise or strong air conditioning units.

1. In the Sound Recording menu, locate Wind Filter.

2. Set this to On when shooting outdoors or in environments prone to low-frequency noise.

Attenuator (ATT)

The Attenuator is an electronic pad that reduces the strength of the incoming audio signal before it is processed by the camera's preamp. Use this only when recording extremely loud events, such as concerts, loud music, or close-range vehicle noise.

1. In the Sound Recording menu, locate Attenuator.

2. Set this to On if your Rec. Level meter is clipping or staying in the red zone even when the Rec. Level slider is set to its minimum value. The Attenuator prevents the signal from overloading the microphone input.

Step 5: Essential Audio Monitoring

Relying solely on the Level Meter is a common mistake; distortion, interference, and unexpected background noises are only detectable by listening. The 5D Mark IV includes a dedicated headphone jack for monitoring.

1. Connect a pair of reliable, closed-back headphones to the HEADPHONE jack (3.5mm stereo mini-jack) on the left side of the camera body.

2. Use the Headphone Volume control in the Menu (or the Quick Control Screen) to set a comfortable listening volume. This volume only affects your monitoring level, not the recorded volume.

3. Listen to the audio before, during, and immediately after recording the first clip. Listen specifically for:

Hiss or static (indicates poor cable shielding or mic interference).

Pops or clicks (indicates clipping or cable movement).

Unwanted ambient noise (ensuring the microphone is properly aimed or shielded).

Continuous monitoring is the only way to guarantee professional, artifact-free audio capture.

Live View, Touchscreen Control, and Silent Operation

The Live View feature turns the 5D Mark IV into a dynamic screen-based camera, offering advantages in terms of composition, precise focusing, and access to the camera's video capabilities. Mastering Live View also unlocks the speed and efficiency of the built-in touchscreen.

Engaging Live View and Focus Precision

To transition from the optical viewfinder (OVF) to Live View, locate the STILL/MOVIE switch next to the viewfinder.

1. Activate Live View: Move the switch to the icon representing a camera (STILL) for still photography, or the icon representing a movie camera (MOVIE) for video.

2. Start/Stop: Press the large START/STOP button located in the center of the switch to engage the mirror lock-up and display the image on the LCD screen.

3. Focus Method: In Live View, the camera utilizes Dual Pixel CMOS AF directly on the sensor, which is much faster and more accurate than phase-detection AF for screen-based shooting.

4. Precision Check for Stills (Manual Focus Aid): If you are relying on manual focus, or if you want to critically confirm sharpness before capture, use the Magnify button (magnifying glass icon, near the top right of the LCD).

Pressing it cycles through 5x and 10x magnification, allowing you to zoom in on the exact focus point. This step is essential for architecture, macro, or still life photography where ultimate sharpness is required.

Utilizing Touchscreen Control

The 5D Mark IV's articulated screen is a powerful tool for rapid adjustment and focus control, minimizing the need to hunt through menus or use physical dials for every change.

1. Quick Setting Adjustment: When the Quick Control Screen is active (press the Q button), you can use your finger to tap and adjust settings such as ISO, White

Balance, Picture Style, and Metering Mode. Tap the setting icon, and the adjustment screen will pop up.

2. Instant Focus Point Placement: In Live View (for stills) or Movie mode (for video), simply tap the area of the screen where you want the focus point to land.

The camera will instantly move the AF point and acquire focus. This is dramatically faster than manipulating the focus point selector physically, especially when utilizing the Dual Pixel AF for subject tracking.

3. Touch Shutter: In Live View mode, you can activate the Touch Shutter via the settings. Once enabled, tapping the screen not only sets focus but also triggers the shutter release immediately, offering an incredibly fast way to capture specific moments.

Activating Silent Operation

There are many professional situations (weddings, church ceremonies, theater performances, or close-up wildlife photography) where the audible clatter of the DSLR mirror and mechanical shutter is disruptive. The 5D Mark IV offers a specific Silent Shooting mode to minimize operational noise.

1. Access Drive Mode: Locate the Drive/AF Mode button (typically near the top left of the camera body, labeled with a stack of rectangles). Press this button or access Drive Mode via the Quick Control Screen (Q).

2. Select Silent Mode: Cycle through the Drive Modes until you reach one of the Silent options:

Silent Single Shooting (S): The quietest single capture mode. The shutter and mirror cycle is dampened and delayed until you lift your finger from the shutter button.

Silent Continuous Shooting (Qc): Offers a quiet burst rate (slower than standard continuous shooting) while minimizing the mechanical sound.

3. Execution: In Silent Single mode, hold the shutter button down completely to fire the shot, and the camera will delay the mirror reset sound until you release the button. This allows you to control the exact timing of the noise, ensuring it occurs at a less sensitive moment.

CHAPTER 11

Review, Workflow, and Connectivity

The act of capturing an image is only half the creative process. The efficiency with which you manage, review, and transfer your files determines how much time you spend behind the lens versus behind a desk.

For many photographers, the post-capture workflow checking sharpness, confirming exposure, and moving files is a frustrating bottleneck.

This chapter is designed to eliminate that frustration entirely. We will treat the Canon EOS 5D Mark IV not just as a capture tool, but as the powerful workflow hub it is. Mastering efficient image review means you can confidently confirm focus and exposure the instant a shot is taken, preventing disastrous errors and allowing you to adjust settings immediately.

You will learn how to leverage the camera's magnification tools and histogram displays to perform critical quality checks in the field, turning your LCD screen into a professional analysis tool. Furthermore, we will demystify the built-in connectivity featuresWi-Fi and Bluetoothwhich allow for lightning-fast file transfer, immediate sharing, and advanced remote control, saving crucial time when rapid turnaround is required.

By the end of this section, you will have a streamlined, repeatable process for reviewing, organizing, and moving your images, ensuring that you spend less time wrestling with technology and more time maximizing your creative output.

Reviewing Images, Checking Focus, and In-Camera Organization

Once you have captured an image, reviewing it quickly and accurately is essential to confirming your settings were correct. The 5D Mark IV offers sophisticated tools to verify focus and exposure before you move on to the next shot.

Step-by-Step Image Review

1. Press the Playback Button (the button with the triangular arrow icon on the back of the camera).

2. To navigate between captured images, use the Main Dial (located near the shutter button) or the Quick Control Dial (on the camera back). The Quick Control Dial is generally faster for reviewing a large sequence of shots.

3. To jump quickly through hundreds of images, use the Index/Reduce button (upper right of the back of the camera). This will show a grid view of 4, 9, or 36 images simultaneously.

Critically Checking Focus with the Magnify Button

The single most important technical check you can perform in the field is verifying critical sharpness. Relying solely on the small LCD screen is dangerous; use the Magnify button to zoom in to a 100% view.

1. Locate the Magnify/Zoom Button (the button with the magnifying glass icon and the plus sign, located to the left of the Quick Control Dial).

2. After opening an image in playback, press the Magnify button once. The image will zoom in, usually to 5x magnification, centered around the active AF point used during capture.

3. Press the Magnify button again to zoom further, usually to 10x magnification (pixel-level view).

4. Use the Multi-controller (the small joystick near your thumb) to move the zoomed area across the screen. You must move the zoomed box directly over the area of focus, such as the subject's eye, to check for perfect sharpness.

5. If the image appears perfectly sharp at 10x magnification, you can trust the focus. If it looks soft, you know to re-shoot and potentially adjust your AF Case settings or lens technique.

6. To return to the full-frame view, press the Magnify button (or the Index button) repeatedly until the image fits the screen again.

Confirming Exposure Accuracy with the Histogram

The histogram is a graph that plots the distribution of tones (from black on the left to white on the right) in your image. Learning to read it is far more accurate than relying on the brightness of the LCD screen, especially in bright sunlight.

1. While viewing an image in playback, press the INFO button repeatedly. This cycles through various display views (basic info, shooting data, detailed data).

2. Continue pressing INFO until the histogram display appears. The 5D Mark IV shows two histogram types:

Luminosity Histogram: This is the primary gray graph, showing the overall brightness of the image. For a properly exposed image, the peak of the graph should be centrally located, though this depends entirely on the scene.

RGB Histograms: These small, colored graphs show the distribution of Red, Green, and Blue channels. These are vital for detecting color clipping (e.g., in vivid sunsets, where one color channel might be blown out even if the overall luminosity looks fine).

3. Check for Clipping: Look for the graph to "pile up" against the far left (pure black/shadow clipping) or the far

right (pure white/highlight clipping). If the graph touches the far right edge, you have lost detail in the highlights.

4. Highlight Alert: When the histogram is displayed, areas of the image that are completely overexposed (clipped highlights) will blink or flash black-and-white.

This is a critical visual cue indicating you must dial down your exposure (reduce ISO, increase shutter speed, or stop down aperture).

In-Camera Organization: Ratings and Protect

Using the in-camera organization tools allows you to tag images for quick sorting later in post-processing software like Adobe Lightroom or Capture One. This is an essential step for efficient workflow.

Applying Image Ratings (Stars)

Rating your images in-camera saves immense time by pre-selecting your keepers before importing them to your computer.

1. Press the Playback Button and select the image you wish to rate.

2. Press the SET button. This often brings up a Quick Control menu, or you may need to access the menu:

- Go to Playback Menu 1.
- Select Rating.

3. Use the Multi-controller or Quick Control Dial to select the desired rating (1 to 5 stars).

4. You can jump to the next or previous image and apply a rating without leaving the screen.

5. All major post-processing software recognizes these ratings, allowing you to instantly filter for your 4-star and 5-star keepers after import.

Using the Protect Feature (Locking Files): The Protect feature locks an image file to prevent accidental deletion, particularly if you use the "Erase All Images on Card" function.

1. Select the image you want to protect during playback.

2. Go to Playback Menu 1.

3. Select Protect Images.

4. Select the image and press SET to apply the protective lock icon.

5. A small key icon will appear on the image display. Protected files can only be deleted by formatting the card

completely, or by manually removing the protection status. This provides a safety net for your most important captures.

Wi-Fi, Bluetooth, and Remote Shooting Made Simple

The Canon EOS 5D Mark IV includes robust Wi-Fi capabilities that allow for streamlined image transfer and full remote control via a smartphone or tablet. Utilizing this feature dramatically speeds up your workflow, especially when you need to quickly review focus on a larger screen or trigger the camera remotely.

Connecting the Camera and Smartphone (Wi-Fi Setup)

1. Preparation: On your smartphone or tablet, download and install the free Canon Camera Connect application from the appropriate app store (iOS App Store or Google Play).

2. Activate Camera Wi-Fi: Press the MENU button on the 5D Mark IV. Navigate to the yellow Set-up tab (Wrench icon) and select 'Wireless communication settings' -> 'Wi-Fi/Bluetooth connection'.

3. Select Connection Type: Select 'Connect to smartphone'. If this is your first time, the camera may prompt you to

register a nickname. Next, select 'Easy connection'. The camera will display a Network Name (SSID) and an encryption key (password).

4. Connect the Smart Device: On your smartphone, go to your Wi-Fi settings and locate the network name displayed on the camera's LCD screen. Connect to this network using the provided password.

5. Launch the App: Open the Canon Camera Connect app on your smartphone. The app should automatically detect the camera connection.

Tap the camera's name to register and establish the link. The camera display will confirm that the Wi-Fi connection is established.

Functionality 1: Image Transfer and Review

Once connected, select the 'Images on Camera' option within the app.

Immediate Benefit: The primary advantage of transferring images wirelessly is the ability to instantly review your files on a screen significantly larger and higher resolution than the camera's own LCD. This is crucial for verifying critical focus and composition immediately after capture.

Transfer Process: You can browse thumbnails of all images stored on the memory cards. Select individual JPEG files or downsized RAW files, and tap the save button to transfer them directly to your device's photo library.

This is ideal for quickly processing and sharing shots online or via social media without needing a computer.

Functionality 2: Remote Live View Shooting

Select the 'Remote live view shooting' option in the Canon Camera Connect app.

Full Control: Your smartphone now acts as a high-fidelity remote monitor. You will see exactly what the camera sees in real-time. You can adjust critical exposure parameters (Aperture, Shutter Speed, ISO), change the metering mode, and even adjust the focus point simply by tapping anywhere on the live view screen.

Applications: Remote shooting is indispensable for sensitive situations like wildlife photography, long-exposure landscapes (where touching the shutter button introduces shake), and macro photography, allowing you to maintain perfect composition and focus while triggering the shutter from a distance.

CHAPTER 12

Reliability, Maintenance, and Field Readiness

I have dedicated the entire preceding volume to achieving peak technical and creative performance with your Canon EOS 5D Mark IV. You know how to control light, lock focus, and customize your settings for speed.

The final piece of the professional puzzle, however, is reliability. True confidence in the field stems not just from knowing your settings, but from knowing your equipment is physically sound and ready to perform under pressure.

Your 5D Mark IV is a sophisticated tool, and like any high-performance instrument, it requires proper care and preparation to maintain peak functionality. Ignoring routine maintenance or failing to prepare the system correctly for a shoot can lead to image quality degradation, catastrophic data loss, or missed shots due to technical oversight.

This chapter serves as your ultimate guide to preserving the longevity of your investment and eliminating frustrating, avoidable operational failures. We will walk step-by-step through essential maintenance procedures, including safe cleaning and sensor care, address common mistakes that often derail a new user's workflow, and provide a professional field checklista final assurance that when you step out to capture the moment, your Canon EOS 5D Mark IV is as ready as you are.

Cleaning, Care, and Long-Term Camera Health

I. Routine External Maintenance

Regular cleaning is vital to prevent dust and grime from migrating into the lens mount or onto the sensor. Always perform maintenance in a clean, dust-free environment.

Cleaning the Camera Body:

1. Power Down: Always turn the camera off and remove the battery grip (if attached) before cleaning.

2. Remove Loose Dust: Use a clean, oil-free air bulb (not canned air, which can spray propellant) to blow dust and debris away from the seams, dials, and button areas. Focus especially on the viewfinder eyepiece.

3. Wipe Down: Use a clean, dry microfiber cloth to wipe the camera body gently. For stubborn spots on the rubber grips, a cloth slightly dampened with water or a specific electronic cleaning solution can be used sparingly, but ensure no liquid enters the ports or buttons.

4. LCD Screens: Use specialized LCD cleaning fluid and a soft microfiber cloth only. Avoid excessive pressure.

Cleaning the Lenses:

1. Air First: Use the air bulb to remove all loose dust particles from the front and rear elements. If dust remains, proceeding with wiping can cause scratches.

2. Brush: Use a soft lens brush (camel hair or similar) to gently sweep any remaining surface debris away.

3. Lens Fluid: If smudges (like fingerprints or water spots) remain, use a lens cleaning solution applied to a dedicated lens cleaning tissue or cloth (never directly onto the glass). Wipe in a circular motion, starting from the center of the lens and moving outward.

II. Initiating Manual Sensor Cleaning

The Canon 5D Mark IV has an automatic sensor cleaning function that runs when the camera is powered on or off. However, sometimes manual intervention is needed for stubborn spots or professional wet cleaning.

Crucial Safety Warning: Never proceed with manual sensor cleaning unless the battery is fully charged (100%). If the battery dies while the mirror is locked up, the sensor can be damaged or the camera may need service.

Step-by-Step Manual Cleaning Lock-Up:

1. Charge the Battery: Verify the LP-E6N battery is completely charged.

2. Access the Menu: Press the MENU button.

3. Navigate to Setup: Go to the Setup Menu (Wrench Icon), Tab 3.

4. Select Cleaning: Choose the "Sensor cleaning" option.

5. Choose Manual: Select "Clean manually." A confirmation screen will appear.

6. Confirm: Press SET to initiate the process. The mirror will lock up, and the shutter curtain will open, exposing the sensor for cleaning or inspection. The camera display will show a warning: "Shutter open: cleaning manually."

7. Perform Cleaning: While the sensor is exposed, use an air bulb (not canned air) to gently puff air onto the sensor surface to remove debris. Do not touch the sensor surface unless using specialized, approved cleaning swabs and solutions.

8. Exit: Turn the camera power switch to OFF. This will close the shutter and lower the mirror, ending the manual cleaning mode.

III. Storage and Longevity Best Practices

Battery Health:

To maximize the lifespan of your rechargeable batteries (LP-E6N):

Avoid Extremes: Do not expose batteries to extreme heat (like leaving them in a car) or extreme cold for long durations.

Long-Term Storage: If storing batteries for more than a month, try to maintain a charge level around 50%. Storing them fully charged or fully drained degrades the cell capacity over time.

Memory Card Health:

Format In-Camera: Always format your CF and SD cards within the 5D Mark IV using the "Format card" option (Setup Menu, Tab 1) rather than deleting files individually on a computer. Formatting refreshes the card structure, minimizing read/write errors.

Eject Safely: Always safely eject the memory card from your computer before physically removing it to prevent file corruption.

Camera Storage:

Protection: When the camera is not in use, ensure both the body cap and the rear lens cap are securely attached to prevent dust and humidity from entering the body cavity or damaging the rear lens element.

Environment: Store the camera in a cool, dry place, ideally in a camera bag with low humidity. If you live in a high-humidity environment, use small packets of silica gel (desiccant) inside the bag to absorb moisture, which prevents fungus growth on the sensor and lens elements.

Travel: When traveling from cold to warm, humid environments, keep the camera sealed in its bag until it has gradually warmed up to the ambient temperature. This prevents condensation from forming inside the camera body.

Common Mistakes, Quick Fixes, and a Pro Field Checklist

The Five Most Common Operational Mistakes (and How to Fix Them Instantly)

Even with the best preparation, subtle settings can ruin a shot. Here are the five most frequent errors made by new and intermediate 5D Mark IV users, along with their immediate solutions.

1. The Camera Will Not Focus, or Focuses Only Once

Mistake: Leaving the camera set to the wrong Autofocus Mode (One-Shot when the subject is moving, or AI Servo when the subject is completely still).

Quick Fix:

Step 1: Locate the AF Operation Mode button on the top plate (near the shutter button).

Step 2: Press the button and use the Main Dial (near the shutter) to change the mode.

Step 3: Select One-Shot (square icon) for static subjects (landscapes, portraits). Select AI Servo (running icon) for all moving subjects (action, wildlife).

2. Exposure Is Wildly Inconsistent (Too Dark/Bright)

Mistake: Exposure Compensation (EV) was accidentally set and left on, or the Auto Exposure Lock (AE-L) button was pressed and locked the exposure.

Quick Fix:

Step 1: Look at the exposure indicator scale on the top LCD or in the viewfinder.

Step 2: If the scale shows a non-zero value (+2, -1, etc.), rotate the Quick Control Dial (the large dial on the rear of the camera) until the indicator returns to 0.

Step 3: If an asterisk () or "FEL" icon is visible, press the AE Lock button (labeled with the asterisk on the rear of the camera) again to release the lock.

3. The Camera Only Takes One Photo and Stops in Burst Mode

Mistake: The Drive Mode is incorrectly set to Single Shot, or the camera buffer is clogged due to a slow memory card.

Quick Fix:

Step 1: Press the Drive Mode button (near the ISO button on the top plate).

Step 2: Use the Main Dial to scroll until you select High-Speed Continuous (H).

Step 3: If the problem persists, ensure your memory cards (CF or SD) are modern, high-speed cards (UHS-I or UDMA 7 recommended for the 5D Mark IV) to clear the buffer quickly.

4. Dials or Buttons Suddenly Stop Working

Mistake: The photographer has accidentally engaged the Lock switch, which locks the Quick Control Dial and other assignable controls to prevent accidental changes.

Quick Fix:

Step 1: Locate the LOCK switch below the rear Quick Control Dial.

Step 2: If the switch is moved fully to the bottom position (LOCK), move it back to the top (unlocked) position.

5. Indoor Photos Look Too Yellow or Blue

Mistake: The camera's Auto White Balance (AWB) is struggling with complex or artificial lighting, or a fixed White Balance setting was forgotten.

Quick Fix:

Step 1: Press the WB button on the top plate.

Step 2: Scroll the Main Dial to select the appropriate preset for the scene (e.g., Tungsten/Lightbulb icon for indoor incandescent light).

Step 3: For critical color accuracy, perform a Custom White Balance using a gray card or neutral target. (Custom WB procedure is located in the Shoot Menu 3).

The Pro Field Checklist: 7 Steps Before You Shoot

Confidence in the field starts with eliminating technical variables. Before beginning any professional shoot, quickly confirm the following settings using the top LCD and rear display. This process should take less than 30 seconds.

1. Battery Check: Confirm charge level is 90% or higher. Carry a spare.

2. Card Check: Are both memory cards inserted? Are they formatted (Format setting in the Setup Menu 1)? Is the correct recording function (e.g., RAW to Slot 1, JPEG to Slot 2) selected?

3. Exposure Mode: Is the mode dial set to the desired setting (M, Av, or Tv)? Avoid the P or Green Box (Auto) modes.

4. ISO Limit: Check the actual ISO setting, or if using Auto ISO, confirm that the maximum limit is set appropriately for your noise tolerance (e.g., ISO 6400 max).

5. AF Mode & Case: If shooting action, is AI Servo selected? Is the correct AF Case (e.g., Case 3 for erratic movement) engaged? If shooting static subjects, is One-Shot selected?

6. Image Quality: Is the camera set to record the highest quality files required (e.g., L RAW)?

7. White Balance: Is the WB set to Auto (AWB) or the correct preset for the current lighting environment?

CONCLUSION

You have reached the final page of this guide, which means you are now ready to begin the most important part of your journey: creating with total confidence.

You have moved beyond the confusion of technical manuals and the guesswork of unfamiliar menus. You no longer simply know where the settings are; you understand how they interact and, more critically, how to adjust them instantly to capture the scene before you.

Your Canon EOS 5D Mark IV is no longer an intimidating tool, it is an extension of your creative eye, perfectly configured to your unique workflow.

Take the precision you've built in exposure, the reliability you've established in autofocus, and the efficiency you've secured through customization, and turn your focus entirely toward light, composition, and storytelling.

The technical obstacles have been removed. Now, go create. I look forward to seeing the masterful work you produce.

www.ingramcontent.com/pod-product-compliance
Lightning Source LLC
LaVergne TN
LVHW100320210926
848480LV00003B/1200
9798295632303